1 ingredient, 4 ways

1 ingredient, 4 ways

50 ingredients
4 recipes for each
200 great dishes

First published in 2010
LOVE FOOD is an imprint of Parragon Books Ltd

Parragon
Queen Street House
4 Queen Street
Bath BA1 1HE, UK

ISBN: 978-1-4075-9080-6

Printed in China

Cover photography by Charlie Richards
Cover shot styling by Mary Wall
Main ingredient photography by Charlie Richards

Notes for the Reader

This book uses imperial, metric, and US cup measurements. Follow the same units of measurement throughout; do not mix imperial and metric. All spoon measurements are level: teaspoons are assumed to be 5 ml, and tablespoons are assumed to be 15 ml. Unless otherwise stated, milk is assumed to be whole, eggs and individual vegetables, such as potatoes, are medium, and pepper is freshly ground black pepper.

The times given are an approximate guide only. Preparation times differ according to the techniques used by different people and the cooking times may also vary from those given as a result of the type of oven used. Optional ingredients, variations, or serving suggestions have not been included in the calculations.

Recipes using raw or very lightly cooked eggs should be avoided by infants, the elderly, pregnant women, convalescents, and anyone with a chronic condition. Pregnant and breast-feeding women are advised to avoid eating peanuts and peanut products. People with nut allergies should be aware that some of the prepared ingredients used in the recipes in this book may contain nuts. Always check the packaging before use.

garlic

olives

peppers

Introduction   8

Keep me cool   14

Keep me dry   102

Index   222

No shopping needed!

Focusing on just fifty familiar food items, *1 ingredient, 4 ways* shows you how to transform everyday ingredients into knockout meals. The concept couldn't be simpler. The book offers four clear and concise recipes for each ingredient, and you pick and choose according to what's in your refrigerator, freezer, and pantry. The recipes demonstrate how incredibly versatile even the most mundane ingredient can be. For example, in the section on frozen peas you have the option of a summery chilled pea soup, a stylish scallop and pea puree, comforting rice and peas, or a classic French recipe for buttery peas and pearl onions.

Divided into two straightforward chapters, the book opens with *Keep me cool*, which focuses on wholesome fresh produce kept in the refrigerator or freezer. Here you'll find inspiration for anything from broccoli to blueberries, eggs to bacon, or smoked salmon to ground beef. There's plenty of choice for cheese lovers—from homey Macaroni Cheese to Crispy Parmesan-Coated Sea Bass and Deep-Fried Mozzarella—and even some cool ideas for

vanilla ice cream. How about Ice Cream Cookie Sandwiches or Coconut Cream?

Then we move on to *Keep me dry*. Here you'll see how a judiciously stocked pantry is key to successful improvisation. Whether it's pasta or rice, canned tomatoes or tuna, nuts or beans, chili powder or chocolate, these versatile foods and flavorings are ingredients you can use at a moment's notice for a quick snack, or for perking up other dishes. The chapter also includes root vegetables such as potatoes and onions—the backbone of endless satisfying dishes to see you through the week.

This book will inject new life into your cooking. It's perfect for people with action-packed lives, but who want to eat well with minimum fuss. Once you get into the swing of it, you'll have no difficulty coming up with smart ideas for what to cook, whether it's a feast for friends, a family meal, or a peaceful solo supper. There are dishes to tempt both vegetarians and meat eaters, as well as child-friendly meals, delectable desserts, cakes, and tasty snacks.

Take stock!

In budget-conscious times, most of us need to make maximum use of the food we buy, and keep wastage to a minimum. It makes sense to stock up with only what you need for a given period, rather than cramming the pantry and refrigerator with tempting items that you've bought on the spur-of-the-moment, or obscure ingredients that might come in handy should you ever fancy making that dish you enjoyed so much in Oaxaca.

What you keep in stock depends, of course, on whether you live in a bustling city with food stores open around-the-clock, or the countryside where they are few and far between. It also depends on your cooking habits, how many people you cook for, and whether you have laid-back friends who show up for meals unannounced. Whatever your lifestyle this book is packed with all-important know-how for rustling up tasty no-fuss meals.

Plan ahead!

However much you may enjoy food shopping, it can be time-consuming. With careful planning, though, heavy-duty shopping for the pantry or freezer need only be done now and again, allowing you more time for the fun part—choosing items that really are best freshly bought, such as meat, fish and seafood, and most fruit and vegetables.

You'll find it much easier to shop if you have a plan in mind. Before you go, check out what you have in your pantry, refrigerator, and freezer, and take a few minutes to think about meals for the next few days. It's a good idea to go armed with a list—that way unnecessary items won't find their way into your shopping cart. If you're keen on fresh produce, try buying smaller quantities more often so you can enjoy it at its peak.

And don't forget the smaller stores. Seek out and enjoy those neighborhood butchers, fish stores, delis, and cheese stores. They all offer a cornucopia of superb ingredients, perishable and nonperishable, that will make your cooking stand out from the crowd.

Be versatile!

Concentrate on foods that you know you will cook, and that are value for money. A top-notch organic chicken, for example, may not be cheap but it delivers an incredible number of mouthwatering meals. Golden, glistening roast chicken is an unbeatable favorite; alternatively, divide a whole bird into joints and freeze what you don't need—much cheaper than buying separate portions. Chicken breasts are infinitely versatile, and leftovers are a real asset, too. Nuggets from a roast are perfect for a stir-fry or salad. And the carcass can be simmered with onion, carrot, celery, and a handful of parsley to make stock for a great soup or risotto.

Eggs are another must-have. They give soufflés height, add bounce to cakes, and make delectable desserts, such as Lemon Meringue Pie and Crème brûlée. They can be boiled, poached, fried, scrambled, baked, or turned into omelets, each method producing a completely different result.

In the vegetable department, the onion must be one of the most versatile and widely used ingredients. With their deliciously crisp, juicy flesh, white or red onions are a particular boon because they're good both raw and cooked. Slice them into thinnest possible crescents and scatter over salads, or cook them down to a sweet-sharp caramelized mass—wonderful to have on hand as a filling for a richly flavored tart, or for serving with sausages and mashed potatoes.

Tomatoes are another essential. They go into an astonishing number of dishes—salads, soups, and pasta dishes, as well as pizza, tarts, omelets, and curries. Without them, a whole host of everyday favorites would be wiped off the culinary map.

Check the expiration date!

As you browse the book deciding what to cook, check what needs using up next. For example, if you have a package of bacon approaching its expiration date, the book offers you the options of Spaghetti Carbonara, Crispy Spinach and Bacon Salad, Leek and Bacon Tartlets, or Chicken and Potato Soup with Bacon.

Not sure what to do with that jaded bunch of broccoli lurking in the refrigerator? Try it in a warming soup, or on a galette with pancetta and tangy bleu cheese. About to chuck out the remains of a hunk of Parmesan? Grate it and add to corn bread or muffin dough, or use it in a crisp coating for sea bass.

Keep it simple!

As the book shows, the best kind of cooking doesn't depend on exotic and expensive ingredients. Deceptively simple meals can be conjured up from seasonal fresh produce that doesn't cost the earth. Time-honored staples can be transformed by zesty spices, condiments, and good-quality canned vegetables or fish. Make a pasta dish special with a slick of top-notch olive oil, a sprinkling of freshly cracked black pepper, and slivers of juicy garlic. For a subtle sweet-sour tang, trickle syrupy balsamic vinegar over a goat cheese salad, or strawberry semi-freddo. It's simple culinary tricks like these that make everyday dishes shine, and they show that you enjoy cooking, too.

Be creative!

The book also shows you how to get creative with leftovers—a valuable skill in belt-tightening times. Use up stale bread in Panzanella (Italian bread salad), or cooked rice in Homemade Turkey Burgers or Tropical Rice Salad. Cooked potatoes make excellent sautéed potatoes and chili-spiked salmon cakes, and they're also handy for bulking up stews. Soups are great for using up small quantities of leftovers—just blend them in a blender or food processor with some stock or other flavorsome liquid, and season to taste.

Be positive with leftovers and present them with pride, as if they were planned for their own sake rather than having cooked too much. Sometimes it's even worth preparing more of the original dish, so that it can be enjoyed in exciting ways a second time around.

And finally...

For relaxed, stress-free cooking, it's worth taking time out to get organized. French cooks never skip the "mise-en-place" (meaning "everything in its place")—assembling equipment, collecting ingredients, and measuring them before they start to cook. It's a great way of getting started. It means you won't be rummaging in a cupboard with greasy hands for a nonexistent spice, or rushing to the corner store five minutes after closing time. Instead, you'll be enjoying the pleasure of cooking with confidence, preferably with a glass of wine in hand, and giving food and friends the attention they deserve.

Keep me cool

This chapter covers fresh produce that is best stored in the refrigerator or freezer. These foods have a limited shelf life, and will develop off-flavors, and unwelcome or even downright harmful bacteria if not stored correctly.

Many people assume the refrigerator operates at a uniform temperature. The reality is that every refrigerator has cold, cool, and humid zones, which in turn are better for different types of food. It's worth investing in a refrigerator thermometer so you can check out the temperature of different zones.

Raw foods like meat, poultry, and fish and seafood, go in the coldest part, which should run at 32–41°F/0–5°C. Keep them properly covered, and store below other foods to prevent contamination from drips. Dairy produce and eggs are best kept in the cool zone, along with opened jars and bottles labeled "keep refrigerated." Wrap cheeses in wax paper to prevent strong flavors transmitting to other foods. Vegetables and fruit need the humidity of the salad drawer. Keep them loosely wrapped in a paper bag or damp paper towels.

It's a good idea to give your refrigerator a weekly cull, and chuck out anything that's sprouting whiskers, smelling suspicious, or has passed its expiration date.

i. Tomatoes

serves 4

10 oz/280 g buffalo mozzarella, drained
    and thinly sliced

8 tomatoes, sliced

20 fresh basil leaves

½ cup extra virgin olive oil

salt and pepper

serves 8

4 tomatoes, peeled, cored, seeded,
    and finely chopped

8 slices ciabatta, about ½ inch/
    1 cm thick

olive oil, as required

3 large garlic cloves, halved

salt

basil leaves, to garnish

Three-color salad

Arrange the mozzarella and tomato slices on 4 individual serving
plates and season to taste with salt. Set aside in a cool place for
30 minutes.

Sprinkle the basil leaves over the salad and drizzle with the olive oil.
Season with pepper and serve immediately.

Bruschetta

Put the tomatoes in a nylon strainer over a bowl, sprinkle with salt, and let
drain. Meanwhile, heat the broiler to high, with the broiler rack positioned
4 inches/10 cm from the heat.

Brush both sides of all the bread slices with olive oil. Place on the rack
and broil for 2 minutes, or until crisp and lightly browned, then turn and
broil on the other side. Remove the toast from the heat and rub one side
of each with the garlic, pressing down firmly.

Shake the strainer to remove any moisture from the tomatoes, then divide
them between the toasts. Drizzle with a little more olive oil and scatter
basil leaves over, then serve.

3

serves 4

3 tbsp olive oil

2 garlic cloves, finely chopped

10 canned anchovy fillets, drained and
chopped

1 cup black olives, pitted and chopped

1 tbsp capers, drained and rinsed

1 lb/450 g tomatoes, peeled, seeded, and
chopped

pinch of cayenne pepper

14 oz/400 g dried spaghetti

salt

2 tbsp chopped fresh flat-leaf parsley,
to garnish (optional)

Spaghetti alla puttanesca

Heat the olive oil in a heavy-bottom skillet. Add the garlic and cook over
low heat, stirring frequently, for 2 minutes. Add the anchovies and mash
them to a pulp with a fork. Add the olives, capers, and tomatoes, and
season to taste with cayenne pepper. Cover and simmer for 25 minutes.

Meanwhile, bring a large, heavy-bottom pan of lightly salted water
to a boil. Add the pasta, return to a boil, and cook for 8–10 minutes,
or until tender but still firm to the bite. Drain well and transfer to a
warmed serving dish.

Spoon the anchovy sauce into the dish and toss the pasta, using 2 large
forks. Garnish with the chopped parsley, if using, and serve immediately.

4

serves 4

2 tbsp butter

1 tbsp superfine sugar

1 lb 2 oz/500 g tomatoes, halved

1 clove garlic, crushed

2 tsp white wine vinegar

salt and pepper

pastry

1¾ cups all-purpose flour, sifted

pinch of salt

heaping ½ cup butter

1 tbsp chopped oregano,
    plus extra to garnish

5–6 tbsp cold water

Tomato
tarte tatin

Preheat the oven to 400°F/200°C. Melt the butter in a heavy-bottom pan. Add the sugar and stir over a high heat until just turning golden brown. Remove from the heat and quickly add the tomatoes, garlic, and white wine vinegar, stirring to coat evenly. Season with salt and pepper.

Tip the tomatoes into a 9-inch/23-cm cake pan, spreading evenly.

For the pastry, place the flour, salt, butter, and oregano in a food processor and process until the mixture resembles fine breadcrumbs. Add just enough water to bind to a soft, but not sticky, dough. Roll out the pastry to a 10-inch/25-cm circle and place over the tomatoes, tucking in the edges. Pierce with a fork to let out steam.

Bake in the preheated oven for 25–30 minutes, until firm and golden. Rest for 2–3 minutes, then run a knife around the edge and turn out onto a warmed serving plate.

Sprinkle the tarte tatin with chopped oregano, and serve warm.

2. Garlic

serves 4

2 whole garlic bulbs, outer papery layers removed

3 tbsp water

6 tbsp olive oil

2 fresh rosemary sprigs

1 bay leaf

7 oz/200 g soft goat cheese

1 tbsp chopped fresh mixed herbs, such as parsley and oregano

1 French baguette, sliced

salt and pepper

salad greens, to garnish

Roasted garlic with goat cheese

Preheat the oven to 400°F/200°C. Place the garlic in an ovenproof dish. Add the water, half the oil, the rosemary, and bay leaf. Season to taste with salt and pepper. Cover with foil and roast for 30 minutes.

Remove the dish from the oven and baste the garlic with the cooking juices. Re-cover and roast for an additional 15 minutes, or until tender.

Meanwhile, beat the cheese in a bowl until smooth, then beat in the mixed herbs. Heat the remaining oil in a skillet. Cook the bread on both sides for 3–4 minutes, or until golden brown.

Arrange the bread and cheese on serving plates garnished with salad greens. Remove the garlic from the oven. Break up the bulbs but do not peel. Divide between the plates and serve at once. Each diner squeezes the garlic pulp onto the bread and eats it with the cheese.

serves 4

3 lb 4 oz–4 lb 8 oz/1.5–2 kg chicken

½ lemon

40 fat garlic cloves, peeled

2 tbsp olive oil

4 sprigs thyme

2 sprigs rosemary

4 sprigs parsley

1 large carrot, roughly chopped

2 celery stalks, roughly chopped

1 onion, roughly chopped

1½ cups white wine

salt and pepper

crusty bread, to serve

Chicken with 40 garlic cloves

Preheat the oven to 400°F/200°C. Stuff the chicken with the ½ lemon and 4 of the garlic cloves. Rub the chicken with a little oil and some salt and pepper. In a large casserole dish, lay a bed of the remaining garlic cloves, the herbs, carrot, celery, and onion, then place the chicken on top. Pour over the remaining oil and add the wine. Cover with a tight-fitting lid, place in the oven, and bake for 1¼ hours.

Remove the chicken from the casserole and check that it's cooked by piercing with a skewer. The juices should run clear. Cover and keep warm. Remove the garlic cloves from the dish and reserve.

Place the casserole over a low heat and simmer the juices for 5 minutes to make a gravy. Strain, reserving the vegetables.

Carve the chicken and serve it with the vegetables from the casserole. Squeeze the flesh out of the garlic cloves, spread onto the bread, and serve.

3

serves 6

2 whole garlic bulbs

4 tbsp olive oil, plus extra for drizzling

2 lb/900 g pumpkin or butternut squash

2 tbsp fresh thyme leaves, plus extra
  for garnish

2 tbsp butter

1 large onion, finely chopped

1 tbsp all-purpose flour

5 cups chicken stock

heaping ⅓ cup sour cream

salt and pepper

Roasted pumpkin, garlic & thyme soup

Preheat the oven to 375°F/190°C. Take two pieces of foil large enough
to wrap a garlic bulb and place a bulb in the middle of each. Pour
½ tablespoon of olive oil over each, season with salt and pepper, wrap,
and place in a large roasting pan. Peel the pumpkin, then cut into large
chunks. Toss the chunks in the remaining olive oil, some salt and pepper,
and half of the thyme leaves. Place in the roasting pan in a single layer
and roast, uncovered, for 1 hour.

Meanwhile, place a large heavy-bottom saucepan over medium heat,
add the butter, and melt. Add the onion and cook, stirring occasionally,
until softened. Add the flour and cook it through for 2 minutes. Add the
stock, a few spoonfuls at a time to begin with, then add all of it.

When the pumpkin has browned remove it from the oven, add to the
stock, bring to a simmer, and simmer for 10 minutes. Open the garlic
packages and let cool. When cool enough to touch, break up the bulbs,
place the cloves on a cutting board, and press down on each until the
softened garlic presses out.

Remove the soup from the heat and carefully blend in small batches in a
food processor with the garlic and the remaining thyme.

Pour into mugs and drop a spoonful of sour cream on top. Drizzle a little
oil over each, garnish with thyme and serve.

4

serves 4

2 lb 4 oz/1 kg small waxy
    potatoes, sliced

2 tbsp olive oil

3 garlic cloves, peeled

5½ oz/150 g bacon lardons

2⅓ cups heavy cream

2 tbsp fresh thyme leaves

7 oz/200 g Reblochon cheese or any other
    good melting cheese, sliced

salt and pepper

crusly bread, to serve

Potato, bacon & garlic gratin

Preheat the oven to 350°F/180°C. Cook the potato slices in a large saucepan of lightly salted boiling water for 10–15 minutes, or until just tender. Drain.

Heat the oil in a large skillet over medium heat. Hit the garlic cloves with the back of a sturdy knife to split them and add to the skillet. Add the bacon lardons and cook for 3–4 minutes, or until just cooked. Add the potato slices, season and cook for 3–4 minutes. Pour in the cream, then add the thyme leaves and stir well.

Transfer the mixture to a gratin dish and top with the cheese slices. Bake in the preheated oven for 20 minutes, or until golden and bubbling. Serve with the crusty bread.

3. Blueberries

serves 2

2 English muffins
4 lean bacon slices
1 cup blueberries
2 tsp maple syrup or honey

Toasted muffins with blueberries & bacon

Preheat the broiler to medium–high. Slice the muffins in half horizontally and place them, cut sides down, on the rack in the broiler pan.

Lay the bacon on the rack and cook until the tops of the muffins are toasted and the bacon is lightly cooked on one side.

Turn the muffins and divide the blueberries among the bottom halves. Invert the bacon onto the blueberries, covering them completely. Cook for an additional 2 minutes, removing the top halves as soon as they are toasted and the bottom halves when the bacon is browned and crisp.

Place the muffin bases on warmed plates, drizzle with maple syrup, and add the muffin tops. Serve at once.

makes 12

heaping 1½ cups all-purpose flour
1 tsp baking soda
¼ tsp salt
1 tsp allspice
generous ½ cup superfine sugar
3 egg whites
3 tbsp margarine
⅔ cup thick plain yogurt or blueberry-
   flavored yogurt
1 tsp vanilla extract
¾ cup fresh blueberries

Blueberry & vanilla muffins

Preheat the oven to 375°F/190°C. Place 12 muffin paper liners in a muffin pan.

Sift the flour, baking soda, salt, and half of the allspice into a large mixing bowl. Add 6 tablespoons of the superfine sugar and mix together.

In a separate bowl, whisk the egg whites together. Add the margarine, yogurt, and vanilla extract and mix together well, then stir in the blueberries until thoroughly mixed. Add to the flour mixture, then gently stir together until just combined. Do not overstir the batter—it is fine for it to be a little lumpy.

Divide the muffin batter evenly among the paper liners (they should be about two-thirds full). Mix the remaining sugar with the remaining allspice, then sprinkle the mixture over the muffins.

Bake in the preheated oven for 25 minutes, or until risen and golden. Remove the muffins from the oven and serve warm, or place them on a wire rack and let cool.

3

makes 9 squares

scant ¾ cup butter, softened, plus extra for greasing

2 eggs

heaping ¾ cup superfine sugar

1¼ cups self-rising flour, sifted

⅓ cup milk

finely grated zest of 1 lemon

1½ cups blueberries

syrup

4 ripe passion fruit

1 cup confectioners' sugar, plus extra, sifted, for dusting

Blueberry & passion fruit drizzle squares

Preheat the oven to 375°F/190°C. Grease and line the bottom of a 9-inch/23-cm square cake pan.

Whisk the butter, eggs, and sugar until pale and fluffy. Fold in the flour lightly and evenly. Stir in the milk, lemon zest, and 1¼ cups of the blueberries. Spread into the cake pan. Bake in the preheated oven for 25–30 minutes, until firm and golden brown. Remove from the oven and let cool in the pan.

Meanwhile, make the syrup. Scoop the pulp from the passion fruit and rub through a strainer. Discard the seeds. Place the confectioners' sugar and passionfruit juice in a saucepan and heat gently, stirring, until the sugar dissolves.

Prick the warm cake with a fork, and spoon the syrup evenly over the surface. Let the cake cool completely in the pan, then cut into 9 squares and decorate with the remaining blueberries.

4

makes about 3 lb 5 oz/1.5 kg

4 cups blueberries
1 cup freshly squeezed orange juice
2 whole star anise
1 cinnamon stick, lightly bruised
2½ cups granulated sugar
¾ cup liquid pectin

Spicy blueberry & cinnamon jam

Place the blueberries in a large pan with the orange juice. Tie the spices up in a small piece of cheesecloth and add to the pan, then simmer over gentle heat for 20 minutes, or until very soft.

Add the sugar and cook gently, stirring occasionally, until the sugar has completely dissolved. Bring to a boil and boil for 3 minutes, then remove from the heat and stir in the pectin. Let cool slightly.

Discard the spices, then spoon into warmed sterilized jars and cover the tops with wax disks.

When completely cold, cover with cellophane or lids, then label and store in a cool place.

4. Jalapeño Chiles

serves 4

14 oz/400 g potatoes,
  cut into chunks

14 oz/400 g skinless salmon fillet

2 tbsp mayonnaise

1 egg, beaten

dash of milk, if needed

2 jalapeño chiles, seeded and finely
  chopped

1 small bunch fresh cilantro leaves

all-purpose flour, for dusting

1 tbsp olive oil

salt and pepper

serves 6

6 oz/175 g tortilla chips

14 oz/400 g canned refried beans,
  warmed

2 tbsp jalapeño chiles,
  finely chopped

7 oz/200 g canned or jarred pimentos
  or roasted bell peppers, drained
  and finely sliced

1 cup grated Gruyère cheese

1 cup grated cheddar cheese

salt and pepper

Salmon & jalapeño fish cakes

Cook the potatoes in a large saucepan of lightly salted boiling water for 15 minutes, or until tender.

Meanwhile, lightly poach the salmon fillet in a saucepan of gently simmering water for 5–6 minutes (if in one piece), or until just cooked but still moist. Alternatively, cut into 4 equal-size pieces and cook in a microwave oven on medium heat for 3 minutes, then turn the pieces around so that the cooked parts are in the center, and cook for an additional 1–2 minutes—the fish should be lightly cooked. Using a fork, flake the flesh into a bowl.

Drain the potatoes, then return to the saucepan and, while still warm, roughly mash with a fork, adding the mayonnaise, egg, and milk, if needed—the mixture must remain firm, so only add the milk if necessary. Stir in the chiles, cilantro leaves, and salt and pepper to taste, then lightly mix in the salmon flakes.

With floured hands, form the mixture into 8 small patties. Heat the oil in a large, nonstick skillet over medium–high heat, then add the patties and cook for 5 minutes on each side, or until golden brown. Carefully remove with a spatula and serve immediately.

Nachos with jalapeños & cheese

Preheat the oven to 400°F/200°C.

Spread the tortilla chips out over the bottom of a large, shallow, ovenproof dish or roasting pan. Cover with the warmed refried beans. Sprinkle over the chiles and pimentos and season to taste with salt and pepper.

Mix the cheeses together in a bowl and sprinkle on top. Bake in the preheated oven for 5–8 minutes, or until the cheese is bubbling and melted. Serve immediately.

3

makes 12

filling

12 fresh jalapeño chiles

2 tbsp sesame seeds

2 tsp ground cumin

2 tsp amchoor powder, plus extra
   for garnish

2 tbsp minced canned chipotle
   chiles in adobo sauce

2 tsp fresh lime juice

2 tsp water

large pinch of salt

batter

2 cups chickpea flour

2 tbsp rice flour

½ tsp ground turmeric

¼ tsp baking soda

¼ tsp salt

1½ cups water

vegetable oil, for frying

amchoor powder and salt,
   for sprinkling

Jalapeño bhajis

Make a slit down the length of the jalapeños and halfway around the tops just under the stems. Carefully open up the jalapeños and remove the seeds and membranes using the back of a small spoon. Set aside. Place the sesame seeds in a spice grinder and grind to a fine paste. Transfer to a bowl, add the cumin, amchoor powder, chipotles, lime juice, water, and salt and mix together.

To make the batter, whisk together the chickpea flour, rice flour, turmeric, baking soda, and salt in a medium bowl. Whisk in the water until smooth.

In a medium saucepan, heat 6 inches/15 cm of oil to 375°F/190°C. Coat the inside of each jalapeño with about 1 teaspoon of the filling. Top with a very thin coating of the batter (this prevents the filling from leaking out), then dip the jalapeños in the batter, turning to evenly coat. Remove from the batter, letting any excess drip off.

Fry the jalapeños, one or two at a time, for about 5 minutes, until nicely browned and crisp. Remove with a slotted spoon and place on paper towels to drain. Sprinkle with amchoor powder and salt and serve immediately.

4

serves 4

1 small wedge watermelon,
about 4 oz/115 g

2 blood oranges, or 1 red grapefruit

1–2 fresh jalapeño chiles

2 tsp honey

¼ cup preserved ginger, drained, with
2–3 tsp syrup from the jar reserved

1 tbsp chopped fresh mint

Tropical salsa

Peel and seed the watermelon and finely chop the flesh. Put in a bowl.

Working over the bowl to catch the juices, peel the oranges, removing
and discarding all the bitter white pith. Separate into segments, chop the
flesh, and add to the watermelon.

Cut the chiles in half, remove and discard the seeds and membrane,
and finely chop. Add to the fruit with the honey. Stir well.

Finely chop the ginger and add to the bowl with the ginger syrup.
Add the mint and stir well. Transfer the salsa to a serving bowl. Lightly
cover and let stand in a cool place, but not the refrigerator, for 30 minutes
to let the flavors develop. Stir again and serve.

5. Ground Beef

serves 4

1 lb 7 oz/650 g fresh ground beef

1 red bell pepper, seeded and finely
    chopped

1 garlic clove, finely chopped

2 small red chiles, seeded and finely
    chopped

1 tbsp chopped fresh basil

½ tsp ground cumin

salt and pepper

sprigs of fresh basil, to garnish

hamburger buns, to serve

Beef burgers

Preheat the broiler to medium–high. Put the ground beef, red bell
pepper, garlic, chiles, chopped basil, and cumin into a bowl and mix
until well combined. Season with salt and pepper. Using your hands,
form the mixture into burger shapes.

Cook the burgers over hot coals or under the broiler for 5–8 minutes
on each side, or until cooked through. Garnish with sprigs of basil
and serve in hamburger buns.

serves 2

3 tbsp olive oil

3 onions, finely chopped

3 garlic cloves, crushed

2 heaped tsp dried mixed herbs or
    oregano

1 lb/450 g fresh ground beef

1 large egg, beaten

salt and pepper

2–3 tbsp freshly grated Parmesan or
    mozzarella cheese, for serving

tomato sauce

14 oz/400 g canned chopped
    tomatoes

1 tbsp tomato paste

pinch of light brown sugar

Meatballs

Heat 2 tablespoons of the oil in a saucepan over medium heat, then
add the onions and cook, stirring occasionally, for 5 minutes, or until
transparent. Add the garlic and cook, stirring, for an additional minute,
then stir in the herbs. Transfer half the contents of the saucepan to a bowl
and let cool slightly.

To make the tomato sauce, add all the sauce ingredients, with a very little
salt and pepper, to the saucepan, then stir well and bring to a simmer.
Simmer for 20–30 minutes, stirring once or twice, until you have a rich
sauce. Meanwhile, stir the ground beef, egg, and a little salt and pepper
to taste into the onion mixture in the bowl. Combine thoroughly and then
form into 16 small balls.

When the tomato sauce is nearly ready, heat the remaining oil in a
nonstick skillet over medium–high heat. Add the meatballs and cook,
turning a few times, for 5–6 minutes, or until golden on all sides and
cooked through. Serve with the tomato sauce, with the cheese
sprinkled over.

3

serves 4

2 tbsp olive oil

1 tbsp butter

1 small onion, finely chopped

1 carrot, finely chopped

1 celery stalk, finely chopped

¾ cup diced mushrooms

8 oz/225 g fresh ground beef

2¾ oz/75 g lean bacon or ham, diced

2 chicken livers, chopped

2 tbsp tomato paste

½ cup dry white wine

½ tsp freshly grated nutmeg

1¼ cup chicken stock

½ cup heavy cream

salt and pepper

2 tbsp chopped fresh parsley, to garnish

freshly grated Parmesan cheese, to serve

Bolognese sauce

Heat the oil and butter in a large pan over medium heat. Add the onion, carrot, celery, and mushrooms to the pan, then fry until softened. Add the beef and bacon to the pan and fry until the beef is evenly browned.

Stir in the chicken livers and tomato paste and cook for 2–3 minutes. Pour in the wine and season with salt and pepper and the nutmeg. Add the stock. Bring to a boil, then cover and simmer gently over low heat for 1 hour. Stir in the cream and simmer, uncovered, until reduced.

Transfer to serving plates, garnish with the parsley and serve with the cheese.

4

serves 4

2 tbsp olive oil

2 oz/55 g pancetta, chopped

1 onion, chopped

1 garlic clove, finely chopped

8 oz/225 g fresh ground beef

2 celery stalks, chopped

2 carrots, chopped

pinch of sugar

½ tsp dried oregano

14 oz/400 g canned chopped
   tomatoes

2 tsp Dijon mustard

1¼ cups grated cheddar cheese

1¼ cups hot Béchamel Sauce

8 oz/225 g dried lasagna sheets

1 cup freshly grated Parmesan
   cheese, plus extra for sprinkling

salt and pepper

Lasagna

Preheat the oven to 375°F/190°C. Heat the olive oil in a large,
heavy-bottom pan. Add the pancetta and cook over medium heat,
stirring occasionally, for 3 minutes, or until the fat starts to run. Add
the onion and garlic and cook, stirring occasionally, for 5 minutes,
or until softened.

Add the beef and cook, breaking it up with a wooden spoon, until
browned all over. Stir in the celery and carrots and cook for 5 minutes.
Season to taste with salt and pepper. Add the sugar, oregano, and
tomatoes and their can juices. Bring to a boil, reduce the heat, and
simmer for 30 minutes.

Meanwhile, bring a large pot of lightly salted water to a boil, add the
pasta, and cook according to the package instructions, until tender but
still firm to the bite. Drain, refresh in cold water, and drain again.

To make the cheese sauce, stir the mustard and cheddar cheese into the
hot Béchamel Sauce.

In a large, rectangular ovenproof dish, make alternate layers of meat
sauce, lasagna sheets, and Parmesan cheese. Pour the cheese sauce
over the layers, covering them completely, and sprinkle with Parmesan
cheese. Bake in the preheated oven for 30 minutes, or until golden brown
and bubbling. Serve immediately.

6. Chicken Breasts

serves 4

2 tbsp olive oil

2 celery stalks, chopped

1 large onion, chopped

2 sprigs fresh thyme

4 carrots, diced

2 parsnips, diced

½ large turnip or celeriac,
roughly chopped

5½ cups fresh chicken stock

3 skinless, boneless chicken breasts,
about 6 oz/175 g each, cubed

handful fresh parsley, chopped

2 tbsp lemon juice

salt and pepper

crusty bread and butter, to serve

Chicken soup

Pour the olive oil into a large, heavy-bottom saucepan. Add the celery and onion and gently fry for about 15 minutes, until softened.

Add the thyme, carrots, parsnips, and turnip and cook for an additional 5 minutes. Add the stock and chicken and simmer for about 20 minutes. Check that the vegetables are tender, then add the parsley and lemon juice, check the seasoning, and serve with crusty bread and butter.

serves 4

3¾ cups canned coconut milk

heaping ¾ cup chicken stock

2–3 tbsp laksa paste

3 skinless, boneless chicken
breasts, about 6 oz/175 g each,
sliced into strips

18 cherry tomatoes, halved

3 cups sugar snap peas, diagonally
halved

7 oz/200 g dried rice noodles

1 bunch fresh cilantro,
coarsely chopped

Chicken laksa

Pour the coconut milk and stock into a saucepan and stir in the laksa paste. Add the chicken strips and simmer for 10–15 minutes over gentle heat, or until the chicken is cooked through.

Stir in the tomatoes, sugar snap peas, and noodles. Simmer for an additional 2–3 minutes. Stir in the cilantro and serve immediately.

3

serves 4

3 tbsp olive oil

2 leeks, sliced

2 garlic cloves, sliced

2 large skinless, boneless chicken breasts, about 6 oz/175 g each, cut into bite-size pieces

2 sweet potatoes, peeled and cut into chunks

2 parsnips, scrubbed and sliced

1 red bell pepper, seeded and cut into strips

1 yellow bell pepper, seeded and cut into strips

9 oz/250 g mixed wild mushrooms, wiped

14 oz/400 g tomatoes, coarsely chopped

4 cups cooked white long-grain rice

1 small bunch fresh parsley, chopped

heaping 1 cup grated sharp cheddar cheese

salt and pepper

Chicken & vegetable casserole

Preheat the oven to 350°F/180°C.

Heat the oil in a large skillet over medium heat, then add the leeks and garlic and cook, stirring frequently, for 3–4 minutes, or until softened. Add the chicken and cook, stirring frequently, for 5 minutes. Add the sweet potatoes and parsnips and cook, stirring frequently, for 5 minutes, or until golden and beginning to soften. Add the bell peppers and mushrooms and cook, stirring frequently, for 5 minutes. Stir in the tomatoes, rice, and parsley and season to taste with salt and pepper.

Spoon the mixture into an ovenproof dish. Scatter over the cheddar cheese and bake in the preheated oven for 20–25 minutes. Serve immediately.

serves 4

4 skinless, boneless chicken breasts, about 5 oz/140 g each

4 tsp Cajun seasoning

2 tsp corn oil (optional)

1 ripe mango, peeled, seeded, and cut into thick slices

7 oz/200 g mixed salad greens

1 red onion, thinly sliced and cut in half

1 cup diced, cooked beets

¾ cup sliced radishes

scant ½ cup walnut halves

4 tbsp walnut oil

1–2 tsp Dijon mustard

1 tbsp lemon juice

2 tbsp sesame seeds

salt and pepper

Cajun chicken salad with mango & beet

Make 3 diagonal slashes across each chicken breast. Put the chicken into a shallow dish and sprinkle all over with the Cajun seasoning. Cover and let chill for at least 30 minutes.

When ready to cook, brush a stove-top grill pan with the corn oil, if using. Heat over high heat until very hot and a few drops of water sprinkled into the pan sizzle immediately. Add the chicken and cook for 7–8 minutes on each side, or until thoroughly cooked. If still slightly pink in the center, cook a little longer. Remove the chicken and set aside.

Add the mango slices to the pan and cook for 2 minutes on each side. Remove and set aside. Meanwhile, arrange the salad greens in a salad bowl and sprinkle over the onion, beet, radishes, and walnut halves.

Put the walnut oil, mustard, lemon juice, and salt and pepper to taste in a screw-top jar and shake until well blended. Pour over the salad and sprinkle with the sesame seeds.

Arrange the mango and the salad on a serving plate and top with the chicken breast and a few of the salad greens.

7. Bacon

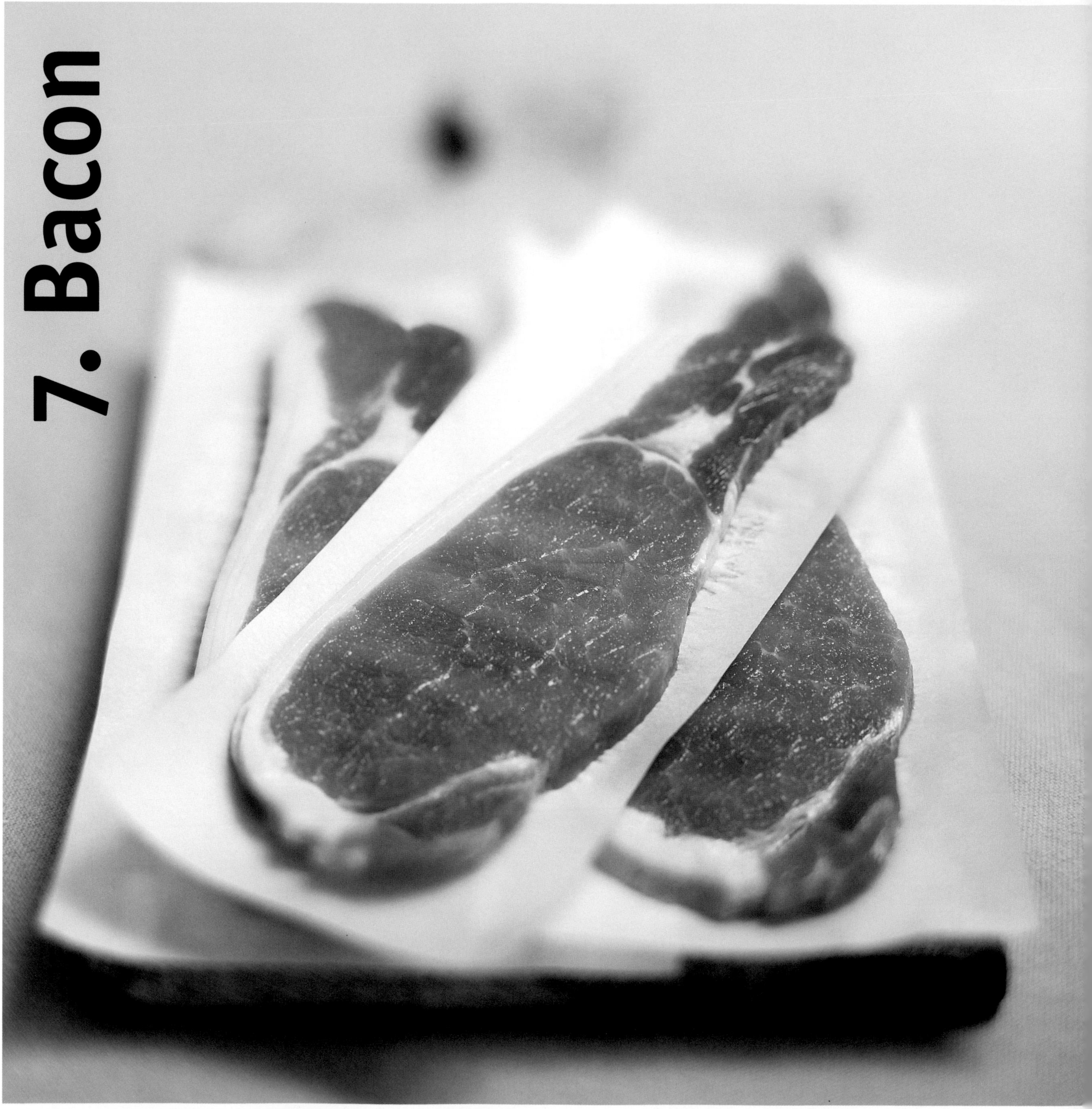

1

serves 4

1 lb/450 g dried spaghetti
1 tbsp olive oil
8 oz/225 g rindless bacon, chopped
4 eggs
5 tbsp light cream
2 tbsp freshly grated Parmesan cheese
salt and pepper

Spaghetti carbonara

Bring a large, heavy-bottom pan of lightly salted water to a boil. Add the pasta, return to a boil, and cook for 8–10 minutes, or according to the package instructions.

Meanwhile, heat the olive oil in a heavy-bottom skillet. Add the bacon and cook over medium heat, stirring frequently, for 8–10 minutes.

Beat the eggs with the cream in a small bowl and season with salt and pepper. Drain the pasta and return it to the pan. Turn in the contents of the skillet, then add the egg mixture and half the Parmesan cheese. Stir well, then transfer to a warmed serving dish. Serve immediately, sprinkled with the remaining cheese.

2

serves 4

4 tbsp olive oil
8 oz/225 g rindless bacon, chopped
1 thick slice of white bread,
    crusts removed, cut into cubes
1 lb/450 g fresh spinach, torn or
    shredded

Crispy spinach & bacon salad

Heat 2 tablespoons of the olive oil over high heat in a large skillet. Add the diced bacon to the skillet and cook for 3–4 minutes, or until crisp. Remove with a slotted spoon, draining carefully, and set aside.

Toss the cubes of bread in the fat remaining in the skillet over high heat for about 4 minutes, or until crisp and golden. Remove the croutons with a slotted spoon, draining carefully, and set them aside.

Add the remaining oil to the skillet and heat. Toss the spinach in the oil over high heat for about 3 minutes, or until it has just wilted. Turn into a serving bowl and sprinkle with the bacon and croutons. Serve immediately.

makes 12

dough

scant 1¾ cups all-purpose flour

pinch of salt

½ tsp paprika

7 tbsp unsalted butter, chilled and diced, plus extra for greasing

filling

2 tbsp unsalted butter

1 tsp olive oil

1 leek, trimmed and chopped

8 strips of bacon, diced

2 eggs, beaten

⅔ cup heavy cream

1 tsp snipped fresh chives

salt and pepper

Leek & bacon tartlets

Lightly grease a 3-inch/7.5-cm, 12-cup muffin pan with butter. Sift the flour, salt, and paprika into a bowl and rub in the remaining butter until the mixture resembles breadcrumbs. Add a little cold water to bring the dough together. Knead the dough briefly on a floured work surface.

Divide the dough in half. Roll out 1 piece of dough and, using a 3½-inch/ 9-cm plain cutter, cut out 6 rounds, then roll each round into a 4½-inch/12-cm round. Repeat with the other half of the dough until you have 12 rounds, then use to line the muffin pan. Cover and chill in the refrigerator for 30 minutes.

Meanwhile, preheat the oven to 400°F/200°C. To make the filling, melt the butter with the oil in a nonstick skillet over a medium heat, add the leek, and cook for 5 minutes, until soft. Remove with a slotted spoon and set aside. Add the chopped bacon to the skillet and cook until crisp. Remove and drain on paper towels.

Line the pastry shells with baking paper and pie weights or dried beans and bake in the preheated oven for 10 minutes. Whisk the eggs and cream together in a bowl, season to taste with salt and pepper, then stir in the chives with the cooked leek and bacon. Remove the pastry shells from the oven and lift out the paper and beans. Divide the bacon-and-leek mixture between the pastry shells and bake for 10 minutes, until the tarts are golden and risen. Transfer to a wire rack. Serve warm or cold.

4

serves 4

1 tbsp butter

2 garlic cloves, chopped

1 onion, sliced

9 oz/250 g bacon, chopped

2 large leeks, sliced

2 tbsp all-purpose flour

4 cups chicken stock

1 lb 12 oz/800 g potatoes, chopped

7 oz/200 g skinless, boneless chicken breast, chopped

4 tbsp heavy cream

salt and pepper

broiled bacon and sprigs of fresh flat-leaf parsley, to garnish

Chicken & potato soup with bacon

Melt the butter in a large saucepan over a medium heat. Add the garlic and onion and cook, stirring, for 3 minutes, until slightly softened. Add the chopped bacon and leeks and cook for an additional 3 minutes, stirring.

In a bowl, mix the flour with enough stock to make a smooth paste, then stir it into the pan. Cook, stirring, for 2 minutes. Pour in the remaining stock, then add the potatoes and chicken. Season with salt and pepper. Bring to a boil, then lower the heat and simmer for 25 minutes, until the chicken and potatoes are tender and cooked through.

Stir in the cream and cook for an additional 2 minutes, then remove from the heat and ladle into warmed soup bowls. Garnish with the broiled bacon and flat-leaf parsley, and serve immediately.

8. Smoked Salmon

serves 4

2 tsp oil

1 large onion, finely chopped

1 large cucumber, peeled, seeded, and
 sliced

1 small potato, diced

1 celery stalk, finely chopped

4 cups chicken or vegetable stock

1⅔ cups heavy cream

5½ oz/150 g smoked salmon, finely diced

2 tbsp snipped fresh chives

salt and pepper

serves 4

9 oz/250 g puff pastry

all-purpose flour, for rolling

1 egg, lightly beaten with 1 tbsp milk

1 small red onion, sliced

3⅓ oz/100 g goat cheese, crumbled

4 slices smoked salmon

pepper

Cold cucumber &
smoked salmon soup

Heat the oil in a large saucepan over medium heat. Add the
onion and cook for about 3 minutes, until it begins to soften.

Add the cucumber, potato, celery, and stock, along with a large
pinch of salt, if using unsalted stock. Bring to a boil, reduce the
heat, cover, and cook gently for about 20 minutes, until the
vegetables are tender.

Allow the soup to cool slightly, then transfer to a food processor
or blender, working in batches if necessary. Puree the soup until
smooth. (If using a food processor, strain off the cooking liquid
and reserve it. Puree the soup solids with enough cooking liquid
to moisten them, then combine with the remaining liquid.)

Transfer the pureed soup into a large container. Cover and
refrigerate until cold.

Stir the cream, salmon, and chives into the soup. If time permits, chill
for at least 1 hour to allow the flavors to blend. Taste and adjust the
seasoning, adding salt, if needed, and pepper. Ladle into chilled
bowls and serve.

Smoked salmon &
goat cheese tarts

Preheat the oven to 400°F/200°C. Roll the puff pastry out to ¼ inch/5 mm
thick on a lightly floured counter and cut into 4 even squares. Place on
an ungreased baking sheet and brush each square lightly with the egg
mixture. Divide the sliced onion evenly between the tarts and top with
goat cheese.

Bake for 20–25 minutes, or until the pastry has risen and is golden brown.
Let cool slightly, then top with the slices of smoked salmon and season to
taste with pepper. Serve at once.

3

serves 4

12 oz/350 g dried linguine

2 tbsp olive oil

1 garlic clove, finely chopped

4 oz/115 g smoked salmon,
  cut into thin strips

1½ cups arugula leaves, torn into pieces

salt and pepper

½ lemon, to garnish

Linguine with smoked salmon & arugula

Bring a large heavy-bottom pan of lightly salted water to a boil. Add the pasta, return to a boil, and cook for 8–10 minutes, or according to package instructions.

Just before the end of the cooking time, heat the olive oil in a heavy-bottom skillet. Add the garlic and cook over low heat, stirring constantly, for 1 minute. Do not allow the garlic to brown or it will taste bitter. Add the salmon and arugula. Season to taste with salt and pepper and cook, stirring constantly, for 1 minute. Remove the skillet from the heat.

Drain the pasta and transfer to a warmed serving dish. Add the smoked salmon-and-arugula mixture, toss lightly, and serve, garnished with a lemon half.

serves 4

7 oz/200 g fresh asparagus spears

1 large ripe avocado

1 tbsp lemon juice

large handful fresh arugula leaves

8 oz/225 g smoked salmon slices

1 red onion, finely sliced

1 tbsp chopped fresh flat-leaf parsley

1 tbsp chopped fresh chives

dressing

1 garlic clove, chopped

4 tbsp extra virgin olive oil

2 tbsp white wine vinegar

1 tbsp lemon juice

pinch of sugar

1 tsp mustard

Smoked salmon salad with avocado

Bring a large pan of salted water to a boil. Add the asparagus and cook for 4 minutes, then drain. Refresh under cold running water and drain again. Set aside to cool.

To make the dressing, combine all the ingredients in a small bowl and stir together well. Cut the avocado in half lengthwise, then remove and discard the pit and skin. Cut the flesh into bite-size pieces and brush with lemon juice to prevent discoloration.

To assemble the salad, arrange the arugula on individual serving plates and top with the asparagus and avocado. Cut the smoked salmon into strips and scatter over the top of the salad, then scatter over the onion and herbs. Drizzle over the dressing and serve.

9. Shrimp

serves 4

¾ cup butter

8 large garlic cloves, finely chopped

2 lb 4 oz/1 kg cooked shrimp, shells on

large handful of fresh flat-leaf parsley, finely chopped

salt and pepper

crusty bread, to serve

Garlic shrimp

Heat the butter in a large skillet or saucepan over low heat. Add the garlic and gently fry for 5 minutes, stirring occasionally.

When the garlic looks like it's about to brown, add the shrimp and gently stir them through the butter. Increase the heat to medium, cover, and cook, shaking the skillet occasionally, for 3 minutes. Add the parsley and cook for an additional 2 minutes. Add plenty of salt and pepper and transfer to a large bowl.

Place in the middle of the table with a bowl for empty shells. Serve with bread for mopping up the butter.

makes 4

1 ripe avocado

7 oz/200 g cooked shelled shrimp

4 wraps, 10 inches/25 cm wide

4 Boston lettuce leaves

dressing

3 tbsp mayonnaise

1 tbsp ketchup

1 tsp Worcestershire sauce

dash of Tabasco

salt and pepper

Shrimp & avocado wraps

Halve the avocado, remove the pit, peel, and cut into eighths. To make the dressing, mix the mayonnaise, ketchup, Worcestershire sauce, and Tabasco sauce together in a bowl. Season with salt and pepper to taste. Add the shrimp and mix well.

Heat a nonstick skillet or grill pan until almost smoking, add the wraps, 1 at a time, and cook for 10 seconds on each side. This will add some color and soften the wraps.

To assemble the wraps, place a lettuce leaf in the center of each wrap, then divide the shrimp in dressing evenly between them. Top with some avocado, then fold in the wraps at the ends, roll up, cut in half diagonally and serve.

3

serves 4

4 oz/115 g cooked shelled shrimp, thawed
    if frozen
4 scallions, chopped
⅓ cup grated zucchini
4 eggs, separated
few dashes of Tabasco sauce, to taste
3 tbsp milk
1 tbsp corn or olive oil
¼ cup grated sharp cheddar cheese
salt and pepper

Shrimp omelet

Pat the shrimp dry with paper towels, then mix with the scallions and
zucchini in a bowl and set aside. Using a fork, beat the egg yolks with
the Tabasco, milk, and salt and pepper in a separate bowl.

Whisk the egg whites in a large bowl until stiff, then gently stir the egg
yolk mixture into the egg whites, being careful not to overmix.

Heat the oil in a large, nonstick skillet and when hot, pour in the egg
mixture. Cook over low heat for 4–6 minutes, or until lightly set. Preheat
the broiler.

Spoon the shrimp mixture on top of the eggs and sprinkle with the
cheese. Cook under the preheated broiler for 2–3 minutes, or until set
and the top is golden brown. Cut into wedges and serve immediately.

4

serves 4

½ iceberg lettuce, finely shredded

⅔ cup mayonnaise

2 tbsp light cream

2 tbsp ketchup

few drops of Tabasco sauce, or to taste

juice of ½ lemon, or to taste

2 cups cooked, shelled shrimp

salt and pepper

paprika, for sprinkling

4 cooked shrimp, shells on, and
    4 lemon wedges, to garnish

thin buttered whole-wheat bread slices,
    to serve

Shrimp cocktail

Divide the lettuce between 4 small serving dishes (traditionally, stemmed glass ones, but any small dishes will be fine).

Mix the mayonnaise, cream, and ketchup together in a bowl. Add the Tabasco sauce and lemon juice and season well with salt and pepper.

Divide the shelled shrimp equally between the dishes and pour over the dressing. Cover and let chill in the refrigerator for 30 minutes.

Sprinkle a little paprika over the cocktails and garnish each dish with a shrimp and a lemon wedge. Serve the cocktails with slices of whole-wheat bread and butter.

10. Eggplant

serves 2

2 tbsp peanut oil or vegetable oil, plus
    extra for deep-frying

2 eggplants, cut into ¾-inch/2-cm cubes

1 bunch of scallions, coarsely chopped

2 garlic cloves, chopped

2 red bell peppers, seeded and cut into
    ¾-inch/2-cm squares

3 zucchini, thickly sliced

1¾ cups canned coconut milk

2 tbsp red curry paste

large handful of fresh cilantro, chopped,
    plus extra sprigs, to garnish

cooked rice or noodles, to serve

Eggplant curry

Heat the oil for deep-frying in a preheated wok, deep pan, or
deep-pan fryer to 350-375°F/180-190°C, or until a cube of bread
browns in 30 seconds. Add the eggplant cubes, in batches, and
cook for 45 seconds to 1 minute, or until crisp and brown all over.
Remove with a slotted spoon and drain on paper towels.

Heat the remaining 2 tablespoons of oil in a separate preheated
wok or large skillet. Add the scallions and garlic and stir-fry over
medium–high heat for 1 minute.

Add the red bell peppers and zucchini and stir-fry for 2–3 minutes.
Add the coconut milk and curry paste and bring gently to a boil,
stirring occasionally. Add the eggplants and cilantro, then reduce
the heat and simmer for 2–3 minutes.

Serve immediately with rice or noodles, garnished with cilantro
sprigs.

serves 2

5 tbsp olive oil

2 onions, finely chopped

2 garlic cloves, very finely chopped

2 eggplants, thickly sliced

3 tbsp chopped fresh flat-leaf parsley

½ tsp dried thyme

14 oz/400 g canned chopped
    tomatoes

1½ cups coarsely grated mozzarella

6 tbsp freshly grated Parmesan
    cheese

salt and pepper

Eggplant gratin

Heat the oil in a flameproof casserole over medium heat. Add the onion
and cook for 5 minutes, or until soft. Add the garlic and cook for a few
seconds, or until just beginning to color. Using a perforated spoon,
transfer the onion mixture to a plate.

Cook the eggplant slices in batches in the same flameproof casserole
until they are just lightly browned. Transfer to another plate.

Preheat the oven to 400°F/200°C. Arrange a layer of eggplant slices in
the bottom of the casserole or a shallow ovenproof dish. Sprinkle with
some of the parsley, thyme, and salt and pepper. Add layers of onion,
tomatoes, and mozzarella, sprinkling parsley, thyme, and salt and pepper
over each layer.

Continue layering, finishing with a layer of eggplant slices. Sprinkle
with the Parmesan. Bake, uncovered, in the preheated oven for
20–30 minutes, or until the top is golden and the eggplants are
tender. Serve hot.

serves 4

2 cups dried penne or other short pasta
   shapes
3 tbsp olive oil, plus extra for brushing
2 eggplants
1 large onion, chopped
2 garlic cloves, crushed
14 oz/400 g canned chopped tomatoes
2 tsp dried oregano
2 oz/55 g mozzarella cheese, thinly sliced
⅓ cup freshly grated Parmesan cheese
5 tbsp dry breadcrumbs
salt and pepper

Stuffed eggplant

Preheat the oven to 400°F/200°C. Bring a large saucepan of lightly
salted water to a boil. Add the pasta and 1 tablespoon of the olive oil,
bring back to a boil, and cook for 8–10 minutes, or according to the
package instructions. Drain, return to the saucepan, cover, and
keep warm.

Cut the eggplants in half lengthwise and score around the insides with
a sharp knife, being careful not to pierce the shells. Scoop out the flesh
with a spoon. Brush the insides of the shells with olive oil. Chop the flesh
and set aside.

Heat the remaining oil in a skillet. Cook the onion over low heat for
5 minutes, until softened. Add the garlic and cook for 1 minute. Add the
chopped eggplant and cook, stirring frequently, for 5 minutes. Add the
tomatoes and oregano and season to taste with salt and pepper. Bring
to a boil and simmer for 10 minutes, until thickened. Remove the skillet
from the heat and stir in the pasta.

Brush a baking sheet with oil and arrange the eggplant shells in a single
layer. Divide half of the tomato-and-pasta mixture among them. Sprinkle
over the slices of mozzarella, then pile the remaining tomato-and-pasta
mixture on top. Mix the Parmesan cheese and breadcrumbs and sprinkle
over the top, patting lightly into the mixture.

Bake in the preheated oven for about 25 minutes, or until the topping is
golden brown.

serves 6–8

2 eggplants
2 red bell peppers
4 tbsp olive oil
2 garlic cloves, coarsely chopped
grated rind and juice of ½ lemon
1 tbsp chopped fresh cilantro
½–1 tsp paprika
salt and pepper
garlic bread, to serve

Eggplant & bell pepper dip

Preheat the oven to 375°F/190°C. Prick the skins of the eggplants and bell peppers all over with a fork and brush with about 1 tablespoon of the olive oil. Put on a baking sheet and bake in the oven for 45 minutes, or until the skins are starting to turn black, the flesh of the eggplant is very soft, and the bell peppers are deflated.

When the vegetables are cooked, put them in a bowl and immediately cover tightly with a clean, damp dish towel. Alternatively, you can put the vegetables in a plastic bag. Let them stand for about 15 minutes, until they are cool enough to handle. When the vegetables have cooled, cut the eggplants in half lengthwise, carefully scoop out the flesh, and discard the skin. Cut the eggplant flesh into large chunks. Remove and discard the stem, core, and seeds from the bell peppers and cut the flesh into large pieces.

Heat the remaining olive oil in a large, heavy-bottom skillet, add the eggplant flesh and bell pepper pieces, and cook for 5 minutes. Add the garlic and cook for an additional 30 seconds. Turn all the contents of the skillet onto paper towels to drain, then transfer to the bowl of a food processor. Add the lemon rind and juice, chopped cilantro, paprika, and salt and pepper to taste, and blend until a speckled puree is formed.

Turn the eggplant and bell pepper dip into bowls and serve with garlic bread. The dip can be served warm or chilled.

ii. Button Mushrooms

serves 4–6

3 tbsp butter

1 onion, chopped

1 lb 9 oz/700 g button mushrooms,
   coarsely chopped

3½ cups vegetable stock

3 tbsp chopped fresh tarragon, plus extra
   to garnish

⅔ cup sour cream

salt and pepper

serves 6

1 lb/450 g button mushrooms

5 tbsp olive oil

2 garlic cloves, finely chopped

squeeze of lemon juice

4 tbsp chopped fresh flat-leaf parsley,
   plus extra sprigs to garnish

salt and pepper

crusty bread, to serve

Creamy mushroom & tarragon soup

Melt half the butter in a large saucepan. Add the onion and cook
gently for 10 minutes, until soft. Add the remaining butter and the
mushrooms and stir-fry for 5 minutes, or until the mushrooms
are browned.

Stir in the stock and tarragon, bring to a boil, then reduce the heat
and simmer gently for 20 minutes. Transfer to a food processor or
blender and process until smooth. Return the soup to the saucepan.

Stir in the sour cream and add salt and pepper to taste. Reheat the
soup gently until hot. Ladle into warmed serving bowls and garnish
with chopped tarragon. Serve at once.

Sautéed garlic mushrooms

Wipe or brush clean the mushrooms, then trim off the stalks. Cut any
large mushrooms in half or into quarters. Heat the olive oil in a large,
heavy-bottom skillet, add the garlic, and cook for 30 seconds–1 minute,
or until lightly browned. Add the mushrooms and sauté over high heat,
stirring most of the time, until the mushrooms have absorbed all the oil in
the skillet.

Reduce the heat to low. When the mushrooms have released their
juices, increase the heat again, and sauté for 4–5 minutes, stirring most
of the time, until the juices have almost evaporated. Add a squeeze of
lemon juice and season to taste with salt and pepper. Stir in the parsley
and cook for an additional minute.

Transfer the sautéed mushrooms to a warmed serving dish and serve
piping hot or warm, garnished with parsley sprigs.

3

serves 4

1lb 8 oz/675 g potatoes, diced
1 tbsp olive oil
2 garlic cloves, crushed
1 green bell pepper, seeded and diced
1 yellow bell pepper, seeded and diced
3 tomatoes, diced
1 cup halved button mushrooms
1 tbsp Worcestershire sauce
2 tbsp chopped fresh basil
salt and pepper
fresh basil sprigs, to garnish

Mushroom, potato & bell pepper hash

Cook the diced potatoes in a large saucepan of lightly salted boiling water for 7–8 minutes. Drain well and reserve. Heat the olive oil in a large, heavy-bottom skillet. Add the potatoes and cook over medium heat, stirring constantly, for about 8–10 minutes, until browned.

Add the garlic and bell peppers and cook, stirring frequently, for 2–3 minutes. Stir in the tomatoes and mushrooms and cook, stirring frequently, for 5–6 minutes. Stir in the Worcestershire sauce and basil and season to taste with salt and pepper.

Transfer to a warmed serving dish and garnish with basil sprigs.

4

serves 8

2 tbsp olive oil

3½ oz/100 g spicy sausage, cut into
    24 slices about ½ inch/1 cm thick

24 button mushrooms

1 green bell pepper, roasted, seeded,
    peeled, and cut into 24 squares

Spicy sausage & mushroom kebabs

Heat the oil in a skillet over medium heat. Add the sausage and cook for
20 seconds, stirring.

Add the mushrooms and continue cooking for an additional 1–2 minutes,
until the mushrooms begin to brown and absorb the fat in the skillet.

Thread a bell pepper square, a piece of sausage, and a mushroom onto
a toothpick. Continue until all the ingredients are used. Serve hot or at
room temperature.

12. Broccoli

serves 4–6

3 cups small broccoli florets

4 tbsp unsalted butter

1 onion, chopped

2½ tbsp basmati rice

8 oz/225 g skinless, boneless chicken breast, cut into thin slivers

scant ¼ cup all-purpose whole-wheat flour

1¼ cups milk

2 cups chicken stock

generous ⅓ cup corn kernels

salt and pepper

serves 6

1 lb 2 oz/500 g broccoli, cut into small florets

scant ½ cup olive oil

1 small clove garlic, chopped

1–2 red chiles, seeded and finely chopped

6 slices country-style bread

salt and pepper

Chicken & broccoli soup

Cook the broccoli in a pan of lightly salted boiling water for 3 minutes, drain, then plunge into cold water and set aside.

Melt the butter in a pan over medium heat, add the onion, rice, and chicken, and cook for 5 minutes, stirring frequently.

Remove the pan from the heat and stir in the flour. Return to the heat and cook for 2 minutes, stirring constantly. Stir in the milk and then the stock. Bring to a boil, stirring constantly, then reduce the heat and let simmer for 10 minutes.

Drain the broccoli and add to the pan with the corn and salt and pepper to taste. Let simmer for 5 minutes, or until the rice is tender, then serve.

Wild garlic & broccoli crostini

Preheat the oven to 375°F/190°C. Cook the broccoli in a large saucepan of salted water for 10 minutes, or until just tender. Drain well and set aside.

Heat about one-third of the oil in a wok or large skillet over high heat, then add the garlic and chile and stir-fry for 2 minutes. Add the broccoli, then season to taste with salt and pepper and stir-fry for 3–4 minutes, or until hot and crisp.

Meanwhile, drizzle the remaining oil evenly over the bread slices and bake in the preheated oven for 10 minutes, or until crisp and golden. Divide the broccoli mixture between the crostini, add a grinding of pepper, and serve immediately.

serves 4

1 sheet puff pastry
heaping 3 cups small broccoli florets,
    halved if necessary
4½ oz/125 g pancetta, diced
1 small red onion, sliced
3½ oz/100 g blue cheese, chopped
pepper
toasted pine nuts, to garnish

Broccoli, pancetta & blue cheese galette

Preheat the oven to 400°F/200°C. Place the pastry on a baking sheet and lightly score a line all around, cutting only halfway through, to within ½ inch/1 cm of the edge.

Steam or boil the broccoli for 4–5 minutes, until just tender. Drain. Fry the pancetta with the onion, stirring, until golden. Stir in the broccoli and season with pepper.

Spread the filling over the pastry, leaving the border clear. Scatter the pieces of cheese evenly over the top.

Bake in the preheated oven for 25–30 minutes, until the pastry is risen and golden. Serve hot or cold, garnished with toasted pine nuts.

4

serves 4

pie dough

1½ cups all-purpose flour, plus extra for dusting

pinch of salt

½ tsp paprika

1 tsp dried thyme

6 tbsp margarine

3 tbsp water

filling

¾ cup cauliflower florets

1 cup broccoli florets

1 onion, cut into 8 wedges

2 tbsp butter or margarine

1 tbsp all-purpose flour

6 tbsp vegetable stock

½ cup milk

¾ cup grated cheddar cheese

salt and pepper

paprika, to garnish

Cauliflower & broccoli tart

Preheat the oven to 375°F/190°C. To make the dough, sift the flour and salt into a bowl. Add the paprika and thyme and rub in the margarine. Stir in the water and bind to form a dough. Roll out on a floured counter and line a 7-inch/18-cm loose-bottom tart pan. Prick the bottom and line with parchment paper. Fill with pie weights or dried beans and bake in the preheated oven, for 15 minutes. Remove the parchment and weights and return the pastry shell to the oven for 5 minutes.

To make the filling, cook the vegetables in a saucepan of lightly salted boiling water for 10–12 minutes, until tender. Drain and reserve.

Melt the butter in a saucepan. Add the flour and cook, stirring constantly, for 1 minute. Remove from the heat, stir in the stock and milk, and return to the heat. Bring to a boil, stirring constantly, and add ½ cup of the cheese. Season to taste with salt and pepper.

Spoon the cauliflower, broccoli, and onion into the pastry shell. Pour over the sauce and sprinkle with the remaining grated cheese. Return the tart to the oven for 10 minutes, until the cheese is golden and bubbling. Garnish with paprika and serve immediately.

13. Zucchini

serves 10–12

4 tbsp butter, diced

2 cups self-rising white flour,
   plus extra for dusting

2 cups self-rising whole-wheat flour

1 tsp salt

1½ tsp mustard powder

1⅓ cups coarsely grated zucchini,
   patted dry

1⅔ cups finely grated Parmesan cheese

1 tsp finely chopped fresh thyme

2 eggs, beaten

¾ cup low-fat milk

pepper

Zucchini & parmesan bread

Preheat the oven to 375°F /190°C. Grease a baking sheet and
set aside. Mix the flours, salt, pepper, and mustard powder in a
large bowl, then lightly rub in the butter until the mixture resembles
breadcrumbs. Stir in the zucchini, Parmesan cheese, and chopped
thyme. Stir in the eggs and enough milk to form a soft dough.

Turn the dough onto a lightly floured surface and knead lightly, then
shape into a 8 inch/20 cm round. Place on the prepared baking
sheet, then cut three fairly deep slashes in the top of the loaf, using
a sharp knife.

Bake in the preheated oven for 40–50 minutes, or until well risen and
deep golden brown. Transfer to a wire rack and let cool. Serve warm
or cold cut into slices, on its own or spread with butter.

makes 20–30

¾ cup self-rising flour

2 eggs, beaten

3–4 tbsp milk

1 large zucchini

2 tbsp fresh thyme

4 tbsp oil

salt and pepper

Zucchini & thyme fritters

Sift the self-rising flour into a large bowl and make a well in the center.
Add the eggs to the well and, using a wooden spoon, gradually draw in
the flour. Slowly add the milk to the mixture, stirring continuously to form
a thick batter.

Grate the zucchini over a few paper towels placed in a bowl to absorb
some of the juices.

Add the zucchini, thyme, and salt and pepper to taste to the batter and
mix thoroughly, for about a minute.

Heat the oil in a large, heavy-bottom skillet. Taking a tablespoon of the
batter for a medium fritter or half a tablespoon of batter for a smaller
fritter, spoon the mixture into the hot oil and cook, in batches, for
3–4 minutes on each side.

Remove the fritters with a slotted spoon and drain thoroughly on
absorbent paper towels. Keep each batch of fritters warm in the oven
while making the rest. Transfer to serving plates and serve hot.

3

serves 4

4 tbsp butter, plus extra for greasing

16 baby zucchini (about 1 lb 2 oz/ 500 g total weight)

⅓ cup all-purpose flour

1¼ cups milk

1 tsp Dijon mustard

1 cup grated sharp cheddar cheese

8 thin slices lean smoked or unsmoked cooked ham

¾ cup fresh white or whole-wheat breadcrumbs

salt and pepper

snipped fresh chives or chopped fresh parsley, to garnish

Cheesy zucchini & ham gratin

Preheat the broiler to medium–high. Lightly grease a shallow, ovenproof dish and set aside. Cook the zucchini in a pan of boiling water for 4–5 minutes, until tender. Drain well, set aside, and keep warm. Meanwhile, melt 3 tablespoons of the butter in a separate pan, then stir in the flour and cook gently for 1 minute, stirring.

Remove the pan from the heat and gradually whisk in the milk. Return to the heat and bring gently to a boil, stirring constantly, until the sauce thickens. Simmer for 2–3 minutes, stirring. Remove the pan from the heat and stir in the mustard and ¾ cup of the cheese. Season to taste with salt and pepper. Cut each slice of ham in half crosswise, then wrap a half slice of ham around each zucchini. Place the ham-wrapped zucchini in a single layer in the prepared dish and pour the cheese sauce evenly over the top to cover.

Combine the remaining cheese and the breadcrumbs and sprinkle evenly over the cheese sauce. Dot with the remaining butter, then place under the broiler for a few minutes, until lightly browned and bubbling. Garnish with snipped chives and serve.

4

serves 4

2 sprays olive oil

1 onion, cut into wedges

1–2 garlic cloves, crushed

2 eggs

2 egg whites

½ cup grated zucchini

1 cup grated carrots

2 tomatoes, chopped

pepper

1 tbsp shredded fresh basil, for sprinkling

Zucchini, carrot & tomato frittata

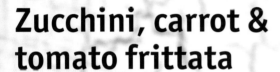

Heat the oil in a large nonstick skillet, add the onion and garlic, and sauté for 5 minutes, stirring frequently. Beat the eggs and egg whites together in a bowl, then pour into the skillet. Using a spatula or fork, pull the egg mixture from the sides of the skillet into the center.

Once the bottom has set lightly, add the grated zucchini and carrots with the tomatoes. Add pepper to taste and continue to cook over low heat until the eggs are set.

Sprinkle with the shredded basil, cut the frittata into quarters, and serve.

14. Frozen Peas

1

serves 3–4

scant 2 cups vegetable stock or water
4 cups frozen peas
4 scallions
1¼ cups plain yogurt or light cream
salt and pepper
2 tbsp chopped fresh mint, to garnish
grated lemon zest, to garnish

Chilled pea soup

Bring the stock to a boil in a large saucepan over medium heat. Reduce the heat, add the peas and scallions, and simmer for 5 minutes.

Cool slightly, then strain twice, making sure that you remove any pieces of skin. Pour into a large bowl, season with salt and pepper, and stir in the yogurt or cream. Cover the bowl with plastic wrap and chill for several hours in the refrigerator.

To serve, remove from the refrigerator, mix well, and ladle into a large tureen or individual soup bowls. Garnish with chopped mint and grated lemon zest.

2

serves 4

4½ cups frozen peas
2 large handfuls fresh mint leaves, roughly chopped
¾ cup butter
12 fat scallops, roes attached, if possible, and removed from their shells
salt and pepper
olive oil, for drizzling

Scallops & pea puree

Bring a large saucepan of water to a boil, then add the peas. Return to a boil and simmer for 3 minutes. Drain the peas, then put them in a food processor with the mint, two-thirds of the butter, and a large pinch of salt. Blend to a smooth puree, adding a little hot water if the mixture needs loosening. Taste for seasoning, cover, and keep warm.

Pat the scallops dry, then season them well with salt and pepper. Melt the remaining butter in a large skillet over high heat. When the butter starts to smoke, add the scallops and sear them for 1–2 minutes on each side. They should be brown and crisp on the outside but light and moist in the middle. Remove the skillet from the heat.

Spread a pool of pea puree on each of four warmed plates and place the scallops on top. Drizzle over a little olive oil, season with salt and pepper, and serve.

3

serves 8–10

butter for greasing

all-purpose flour, for dusting

8 oz/250 g store-bought flaky pastry

3 tbsp cornstarch

1 heaping ⅓ cup superfine sugar

grated rind of 3 lemons

1¼ cups cold water

⅔ cup lemon juice

3 egg yolks

4 tbsp unsalted butter, cut into small cubes

meringue

3 egg whites

¾ cup superfine sugar

1 tsp golden granulated sugar

Lemon meringue pie

Grease a 10-inch/25-cm pie plate. On a lightly dusted work surface, roll out the pastry into a circle 2-inch/5-cm larger than the pie plate. Ease the pastry into the pie plate and press down into the corners. Roll off the excess pastry. Prick the bottom of the shell and chill, uncovered, in the refrigerator for 20–30 minutes.

Preheat the oven to 400°F/200°C. Line the pastry shell with parchment paper and fill with pie weights or dried beans. Bake on a cookie sheet for 15 minutes. Remove the paper and weights and return to the oven for 10 minutes until the pastry is dry and just coloring. Remove from the oven and reduce the temperature to 300°F/150°C.

Put the cornstarch, sugar, and lemon rind into a pan. Pour in a little of the water and blend to a smooth paste. Gradually add the remaining water and the lemon juice. Place the pan over a medium heat and bring the mixture to a boil, stirring continuously. Simmer for 1 minute, until smooth and glossy. Remove the pan from the heat and beat in the egg yolks, then the butter. Place the pan in a bowl of cold water to cool the filling. When cool, spoon the mixture into the pastry shell.

To make the meringue, whisk the egg whites, using an electric mixer, until thick and in soft peaks. Add the superfine sugar, whisking well. The mixture should be glossy and firm. Spoon the meringue over the filling to cover it completely. Swirl the meringue into peaks and sprinkle with the granulated sugar.

Bake for 20–30 minutes, until the meringue is crispy and pale gold (the center should still be soft). Let cool slightly before serving.

serves 6

all-purpose flour, for dusting

16 oz/450 g store-bought flaky pastry

1 lb 10 oz–2 lb 4 oz/750 g–1 kg cooking
   apples

about ⅔ cup brown or white sugar,
   plus extra for sprinkling

½–1 tsp ground cinnamon

1–2 tbsp water

milk or beaten egg, for glazing

Apple pie

Preheat the oven to 425°F/220°C. Roll out almost two-thirds of the pie
dough thinly on a lightly floured counter and use to line an 8–9-inch/
20–23-cm pie plate.

Peel, core, and slice the apples, then mix them with the sugar and
cinnamon and pack into the pastry shell; the filling can come up above
the rim. If the apples are a dry variety add a little water to moisten.

Roll out the remaining dough to form a lid. Dampen the edges of the pie
rim with water and position the lid, pressing the edges firmly together.
Trim and crimp the edges.

Use the pie dough trimmings to cut out leaves or other shapes to
decorate the top of the pie. Dampen the shapes and attach. Glaze the
top of the pie with milk or beaten egg, make 1 or 2 slits in the top, and put
the pie on a baking sheet.

Bake in the oven for 20 minutes, then reduce the oven temperature to
350°F/180°C and cook for 30 minutes, or until the pastry is a light golden
brown. Serve hot or cold, sprinkled with sugar.

16. Cheddar Cheese

 **1**

 **2**

serves 4

9 oz/250 g dried macaroni pasta

4 tbsp butter, plus extra for cooking the pasta

2½ cups milk

½ tsp grated nutmeg

scant ½ cup all-purpose flour

¾ cup grated cheddar cheese

¾ cup grated Parmesan cheese

7 oz/200 g baby spinach

salt and pepper

serves 1

1 croissant

2 thin slices cooked ham, halved

mustard (optional)

2 slices cheddar cheese

1 egg, hard-cooked and sliced (optional)

Macaroni cheese

Bring a large saucepan of lightly salted water to a boil and cook the macaroni according to the package instructions. Remove from the heat, drain, add a small pat of butter to keep it soft, return to the saucepan, and cover to keep warm.

Put the milk and nutmeg into a saucepan over low heat and heat until warm, but don't boil. Melt the butter in a heavy-bottom saucepan over low heat, add the flour, and stir to make a roux. Cook gently for 2 minutes. Add the milk, a little at a time, whisking it into the roux, then cook for 10–15 minutes to make a loose sauce. Add three-quarters of the cheddar cheese and Parmesan cheese and stir through until they have melted in. Add the spinach, season with salt and pepper, and remove from the heat.

Preheat the broiler to high. Put the macaroni into a shallow heatproof dish, then pour the sauce over. Scatter the remaining cheese over the top and place the dish under the preheated broiler. Broil until the cheese begins to brown, then serve.

Ham & cheese croissant

Preheat the broiler to medium–high. Slice the croissant horizontally in half, then lay it, cut sides up, on a piece of foil on the rack in the broiler pan.

Top each croissant with two half slices of cooked ham, overlapping the halves, and spread with a little mustard, if liked. Then top with the cheese, cutting and overlapping the slices to fit the croissant. Broil for about 2 minutes, until the cheese has melted. The croissant will be warmed through and beginning to brown around the edges.

If including the egg, overlap the slices on the bottom half of the croissant. Use a knife to scoop any melted cheese off the foil and onto the croissant, then invert the top in place. Serve at once.

3

serves 4

1 large cauliflower, trimmed and cut
  into florets
3 tbsp butter
heaping ¼ cup all-purpose flour
2 cups milk
1 cup finely grated cheddar cheese
whole nutmeg, for grating
1 tbsp grated Parmesan cheese
salt and pepper

Cauliflower cheese

Bring a large saucepan of lightly salted water to a boil, add the
cauliflower, and cook for 4–5 minutes. It should still be firm. Drain,
place in a hot 1¼-quart/1.4-liter gratin bowl, and keep warm.

Melt the butter in a medium saucepan over medium heat and stir
in the flour. Cook for 1 minute, stirring continuously. Remove from the
heat and stir in the milk, gradually, until you have a smooth consistency.
Return to low heat and continue to stir while the sauce comes to a boil
and thickens. Reduce the heat and simmer gently, stirring continuously,
for about 3 minutes, until the sauce is creamy and smooth.

Remove from the heat and stir in the cheddar cheese and a good
grating of the nutmeg. Taste and season well with salt and pepper. Pour
the hot sauce over the cauliflower, top with the Parmesan, and place
under a hot broiler to brown. Serve immediately.

4

makes 12 biscuits

6 tbsp unsalted butter, chilled, plus extra
for greasing

4 sun-dried tomatoes (not packed in oil)

2½ cups all-purpose flour, plus extra
for dusting

1 tbsp baking powder

½ tsp baking soda

½ tsp salt

½ tsp chipotle powder

½ tsp dry mustard

1 tsp dried basil

1 cup coarsely grated cheddar cheese

¾ cup buttermilk

Cheddar biscuits

Preheat the oven to 400°F/200°C. Grease a baking sheet and set aside.

Soak the sun-dried tomatoes in a small bowl with hot water to cover,
for 10 minutes. Drain, squeeze out excess liquid, and mince. Set aside.

In a large bowl, sift together the flour, baking powder, baking soda, and
salt. Stir in the chipotle powder, mustard, and basil. Cut in the butter
using a pastry blender or rub it in with your fingertips until completely
incorporated. Fold in the cheese and sun-dried tomatoes.

Using a kitchen fork, stir in the buttermilk. The dough will be slightly
sticky. Gather the dough into a ball with your hands and turn out onto a
well-floured work surface. With floured hands, pat the dough ½ inch/1 cm
thick and cut into 12 squares using a floured knife.

Place the squares on the baking sheet with a little space between
them and bake for about 15 minutes, or until well risen and very
lightly browned. Remove from the oven and serve.

17. Parmesan cheese

serves 4–6

2 red bell peppers

4 tbsp olive oil

12 oz/350 g puff pastry, thawed if frozen

all-purpose flour, for dusting

2 ripe but firm tomatoes, thinly sliced

9 oz/250 g ricotta cheese

1 cup grated Parmesan cheese

1 tsp fresh thyme leaves

1 tbsp finely snipped fresh chives

salt and pepper

Summer vegetable & herb tart

Preheat the oven to 400°F/200°C.

Remove the stems and seeds from the bell peppers, and cut the flesh into thin strips. Transfer to a baking sheet and drizzle with half the oil. Season to taste with salt and pepper and roast in the preheated oven for 20 minutes, or until soft. Remove from the oven and let cool while you prepare the pastry shell.

Roll the pastry out on a floured work surface and use to line a 9-inch/23-cm tart pan. Prick the bottom with a fork to prevent the pastry from puffing up.

Scatter the roasted bell peppers evenly over the base, then arrange the tomato slices on top and season to taste with salt and pepper.

Beat the ricotta cheese in a bowl until smooth, then spoon over the vegetables. Sprinkle over the Parmesan cheese, thyme leaves, and chives, then drizzle over the remaining oil. Bake in the preheated oven for 20 minutes, or until the pastry and cheese topping are golden. Serve immediately, or let cool.

serves 4

3 tbsp olive oil

4 sea bass fillets, about 4½ oz/125 g each, skin on and pin boned

juice and grated rind of 1 lemon

1 cup finely grated Parmesan cheese

1 small bunch fresh parsley, finely chopped

salt and pepper

watercress, arugula, or spinach salad, to serve

lemon wedges, to serve

Crispy parmesan-coated sea bass

Preheat the broiler to its highest setting. Brush the broiler pan with a little of the oil and lay the fillets in the broiler pan, skin side down. Drizzle over a little of the remaining oil, then give each fillet a good squeeze of lemon juice and season with salt and pepper.

Mix the lemon rind, Parmesan cheese, and parsley together and scatter evenly over the fish. Drizzle over the remaining oil. Cook under the broiler for 4 minutes, or until the fish is just cooked and golden—the exact cooking time will depend on the thickness of the fillets. Serve immediately with watercress and lemon wedges.

3

serves 16

oil, for greasing
1 cup fine cornmeal
1 cup all-purpose flour
4 tsp baking powder
2 tsp celery salt
½ cup grated Parmesan cheese
2 eggs, beaten
1¾ cups milk
4 tbsp butter, melted
1 bunch scallions, chopped
pepper

Scallion & parmesan cornbread

Preheat the oven to 375°F/190°C. Grease a 9-inch/23-cm square baking
pan. Sift the cornmeal, flour, baking powder, celery salt, and pepper
into a bowl and stir in ⅓ cup of the Parmesan cheese. Beat together the
eggs, milk, and melted butter. Add the egg batter to the dry ingredients
and stir well to mix evenly.

Stir in the chopped scallions and spread the batter evenly into the pan.
Sprinkle the remaining Parmesan over the batter. Bake in the preheated
oven for 30–35 minutes, or until firm and golden.

4

makes 12

oil or melted butter, for greasing (if using)
2 cups all-purpose flour
1 tbsp baking powder
1½ tbsp salt
¾ cup freshly grated Parmesan cheese
⅓ cup pine nuts
2 large eggs
1 cup buttermilk
6 tbsp sunflower oil or melted, cooled
 butter
pepper

topping

4 tsp grated Parmesan cheese
¼ cup pine nuts

Parmesan & pine nut muffins

Preheat the oven to 400°F/200°C. Grease a 12-cup muffin pan or line with 12 muffin paper liners.

To make the topping, mix together the Parmesan cheese and pine nuts and set aside.

To make the muffins, sift together the flour, baking powder, salt, and pepper to taste into a large bowl. Stir in the Parmesan cheese and pine nuts.

Lightly beat the eggs in a large pitcher or bowl, then beat in the buttermilk and oil. Make a well in the center of the dry ingredients and pour in the beaten liquid ingredients. Stir gently until just combined, do not overmix.

Spoon the batter into the prepared muffin pan. Scatter the topping over the muffins. Bake in the preheated oven for about 20 minutes, until well risen, golden brown, and firm to the touch.

Let the muffins cool in the pan for 5 minutes, then serve warm.

18. Muzzirella cheese

serves 4

8 cups vegetable stock

1 tbsp olive oil

3 tbsp butter

1 small onion, finely chopped

2¼ cups risotto rice

½ cup freshly grated Parmesan cheese

4 oz/115 g mozzarella cheese, diced

1 egg, beaten

2 cups fresh breadcrumbs

oil, for deep-frying

salt and pepper

salad greens, to serve

serves 4

1 tbsp butter

4 eggs, beaten lightly

1½ oz/40 g mozzarella cheese, thinly sliced and cut into bite-size pieces

small handful baby spinach, stalks removed

salt and pepper

1 oil-cured red bell pepper, sliced into strips, to garnish

Stuffed rice balls

Bring the stock to a boil in a saucepan, then reduce the heat and keep simmering gently over low heat while you are cooking the risotto. Heat the oil with 2 tablespoons of the butter in a deep saucepan over medium heat until the butter has melted. Add the onion and cook for 5 minutes, until softened. Reduce the heat, add the rice, and mix to coat in oil and butter. Cook, stirring continuously, for 2–3 minutes, or until the grains are translucent. Gradually add the hot stock, a ladleful at a time. Stir continuously and add more liquid as the rice absorbs each addition. Cook for 20 minutes, or until all the liquid is absorbed and the rice is creamy but still firm to the bite.

Remove the risotto from the heat and add the remaining butter. Mix well, then stir in the Parmesan cheese. Season to taste with salt and pepper. Let stand to cool.

Place 1 heaped tablespoon of the cooled risotto in the palm of your hand. Top with a cube of mozzarella cheese, then place another tablespoon of risotto on top. Press together to form a ball, making sure that the filling is fully enclosed. Chill for 10 minutes, then dip in the beaten egg. Drain and coat in breadcrumbs. Chill for 10 minutes.

Heat enough oil for deep-frying in a large saucepan or deep-fat fryer to 350–375°F/180–190°C, or until a cube of bread browns in 30 seconds. Carefully drop the rice balls into the hot oil and cook for 5 minutes, until golden brown. Drain on paper towels. Serve with salad greens.

Mozzarella omelet

Heat a 10-inch/25-cm nonstick skillet over medium–high heat. Add the butter and, when it has melted, pour in the eggs. Season with salt and pepper, then stir gently with the back of a fork until large flakes form. Let cook for a few seconds, then tilt the skillet and lift the edges of the mixture with a spatula, so that the uncooked egg flows underneath.

Scatter the cheese and spinach over the top, and let cook for a few seconds. Once the surface starts to solidify, carefully fold the omelet in half. Cook for a few seconds, pressing the surface with a spatula. Turn the omelet over and cook for another few seconds, until the cheese is soft and the spinach wilted.

Slip the omelet onto a warmed serving dish and slice into segments. Garnish with strips of bell pepper before serving.

19. Eggs

serves 4

1 clove

2 small shallots, peeled, 1 finely chopped

1 generous cup milk

6 black peppercorns

1 bay leaf

2 tbsp butter, plus extra for greasing

scant ¼ cup all-purpose flour,
    plus extra for dusting

4 eggs, whites and yolks separated into
    separate bowls

½ tsp cayenne pepper

9 oz/250 g cooked crabmeat

green salad and crusty bread, to serve

Crab soufflé

Preheat the oven to 400°F/200°C. Push the clove into the whole shallot and place in a small saucepan with the milk, peppercorns, and bay leaf. Heat until just simmering, then remove from the heat and let cool. Strain, reserving the milk and discarding the solids.

Carefully grease a 4-cup, high-sided soufflé dish, then dust with flour, tipping the dish around so that it is completely coated. Discard any excess.

Place a saucepan over low heat and add the butter and the chopped shallot. Cook for about 5 minutes, until the shallot is softened. Add the flour and cook for 3 minutes, stirring, to make a roux. Remove from the heat and add the milk a little at a time, stirring continuously so that it does not become lumpy. Add the egg yolks and cayenne pepper and beat them in thoroughly with a whisk. Add the crabmeat and warm through again, but don't boil. Pour into a mixing bowl.

In a separate bowl, whisk the egg whites until soft peaks form. Add to the crab mixture one-quarter at a time, very gently folding through. Spoon into the soufflé dish, place in the preheated oven, and bake for 25–30 minutes, until golden on top. Do not open the oven door until it is cooked. Spoon onto plates and serve with a green salad and crusty bread.

serves 4

2 tbsp olive oil

2 red bell peppers, seeded and thinly
    sliced

2 zucchini, thinly sliced

1 cup broccoli florets

4 scallions, chopped

2 large tomatoes, seeded and
    chopped

8 eggs

3 tbsp freshly grated Parmesan
    cheese

1 tbsp cold water

salt and pepper

basil, to garnish

Three-color frittata

Heat the oil in a large, nonstick skillet over high heat, then add the peppers, zucchini, and broccoli and cook, stirring, for 3 minutes, or until just softened. Add the scallions and tomatoes and cook, stirring, for 1 minute. Reduce the heat to medium–low.

Put the eggs, Parmesan cheese, and water in a bowl with a little salt and pepper and beat together. Pour the egg mixture evenly over the vegetables in the skillet. Cook, without stirring, for 6–8 minutes, or until the underside of the frittata is cooked and golden but the top is still runny. Meanwhile, preheat the broiler to high.

Put the skillet under the preheated broiler and cook the frittata for 2 minutes, or until the top is cooked and golden, and it is set all the way through. Cut the frittata into 4 wedges, and scatter with the basil for garnishing.

20. Sour Cream

serves 4

1 lb 8 oz/675 g pork tenderloin
2 tbsp corn oil
2 tbsp butter
1 onion, chopped
1 tbsp paprika
2½ tbsp all-purpose flour
1¼ cups chicken stock
4 tbsp dry sherry
⅔ cup sliced button mushrooms
salt and pepper
⅔ cup sour cream

serves 6

juice of 1 lime
3 avocados
2 garlic cloves, chopped
3 scallions, chopped
2 fresh green chiles, seeded and
    chopped
2 tbsp olive oil
1 tbsp sour cream
salt
cayenne pepper, to garnish
tortilla chips, to serve

Paprika pork

Cut the pork into 1½-inch/4-cm cubes. Heat the oil and butter in a large pan. Add the pork and cook over medium heat, stirring, for 5 minutes, or until browned. Transfer to a plate with a slotted spoon.

Add the chopped onion to the pan and cook, stirring occasionally, for 5 minutes, or until softened. Stir in the paprika and flour and cook, stirring continuously, for 2 minutes. Gradually stir in the stock and bring to a boil, stirring continuously.

Return the pork to the pan, add the sherry and sliced mushrooms, and season to taste with salt and pepper. Cover and simmer gently for 20 minutes, or until the pork is tender. Stir in the sour cream and serve.

Guacamole

Put the lime juice into the blender. Halve the avocados and remove the pits. Scoop out the avocado flesh with a spoon straight into the blender.

Add the garlic, scallions, chiles, olive oil, and sour cream and season with salt. Process until smooth. Taste and adjust the seasoning with more salt or lime juice.

Spoon the guacamole into a serving dish. Dust lightly with cayenne pepper and serve with tortilla chips.

3

serves 4–6

6 strips lean bacon, rinds removed,
   if necessary
1¼ cups sour cream
1 bunch scallions, finely chopped
4 tbsp snipped fresh chives

Bacon & sour cream dip

Preheat the broiler. Place the bacon on the broiler rack and broil until well cooked and crisp, turning over once. Transfer to crumpled paper towels to drain and let cool.

Put the sour cream in a bowl with the scallions and chives. Finely chop the bacon and add it to the bowl and stir together. Transfer to a serving bowl, cover, and chill until required.

4

makes 12

oil or melted butter, for greasing (if using)

2 slices canned pineapple in natural juice,
    plus 2 tbsp juice from the can

2 cups all-purpose flour

1 tbsp baking powder

pinch of salt

heaping ½ cup superfine sugar

2 large eggs

scant 1 cup sour cream

6 tbsp sunflower oil or melted,
    cooled butter

1 tsp vanilla extract

Sour cream & pineapple muffins

Preheat the oven to 400°F/200°C. Grease a 12-cup muffin pan or line with 12 muffin paper liners. Drain and finely chop the pineapple slices. Sift together the flour, baking powder, and salt into a large bowl. Stir in the sugar and chopped pineapple.

Lightly beat the eggs in a large pitcher or bowl, then beat in the sour cream, oil, pineapple juice, and vanilla extract. Make a well in the center of the dry ingredients and pour in the beaten liquid ingredients. Stir gently until just combined; do not overmix.

Spoon the batter into the prepared muffin pan. Bake in the preheated oven for about 20 minutes, until well risen, golden brown, and firm to the touch. Let the muffins cool in the pan for 5 minutes, then serve warm or transfer to a wire rack and let cool completely.

21. Vanilla Ice Cream

serves 4

chocolate sauce

2 oz/55 g semisweet chocolate

4 tbsp dark corn syrup

1 tbsp butter

1 tbsp cognac or dark rum (optional)

sundae

⅔ cup heavy cream

4 bananas, peeled

8 scoops vanilla ice cream

¾ cup chopped mixed nuts, toasted

1½ oz/40 g milk or semisweet chocolate, grated

4 ice cream fan-shape wafers, to serve

Chocolate banana sundae

To make the chocolate sauce, break the chocolate into small pieces and place in a heatproof bowl with the corn syrup and butter. Set over a pan of gently simmering water until melted, stirring until well combined. Remove the bowl from the heat and stir in the cognac, if using.

Whip the cream until just holding its shape, and slice the bananas. Place a scoop of ice cream in the bottom of each of 4 sundae glasses. Top with slices of banana, some chocolate sauce, a spoonful of cream, and a generous sprinkling of nuts.

Repeat the layers, finishing with the nuts, then top with the grated chocolate. Top each sundae with a fan-shape wafer.

serves 4

4 tbsp golden raisins

3 tbsp dark rum

4 slices ginger cake

4 scoops vanilla ice cream

3 egg whites

scant 1 cup granulated or superfine sugar

Ginger baked alaskas

Preheat the oven to 450°F/230°C. Mix the golden raisins with the rum in a small bowl. Place the cake slices, spaced well apart, on a baking sheet. Scatter a spoonful of the soaked golden raisins on top of each slice. Place a scoop of ice cream in the center of each slice and place in the freezer until solid.

Meanwhile, whip the egg whites in a large bowl until soft peaks form. Gradually whip the sugar into the egg whites, a tablespoonful at a time, until the mixture forms stiff peaks.

Remove the ice cream-topped cake slices from the freezer and spoon the meringue over the top, spreading to cover the ice cream completely. Bake in the preheated oven for about 5 minutes, until starting to brown.

3

serves 2

1½ cups pineapple juice

⅓ cup coconut milk

⅔ cup vanilla ice cream

5 oz/140 g frozen pineapple chunks

grated fresh coconut, to decorate

2 scooped-out coconut shells, optional,
  to serve

Coconut cream

Pour the pineapple juice and coconut milk into a food processor. Add
the ice cream and process until smooth.

Add the pineapple chunks and process until smooth. Pour the mixture
into scooped-out coconut shells, or tall glasses, and decorate with
grated fresh coconut.

Add straws and serve.

makes about 30

1 cup butter, softened

⅔ cup superfine sugar

1 egg yolk, lightly beaten

2 tbsp finely chopped preserved ginger,
   plus 2 tsp syrup from the jar

2 cups all-purpose flour

3½ tbsp unsweetened cocoa

½ tsp ground cinnamon

about 2 cups vanilla ice cream

salt

Ice cream cookie sandwiches

Put the butter and sugar into a bowl and mix well with a wooden spoon, then beat in the egg yolk, ginger, and ginger syrup. Sift together the flour, cocoa, cinnamon, and a pinch of salt into the mixture and stir until thoroughly combined. Halve the dough, shape into balls, wrap in plastic wrap, and chill in the refrigerator for 30–60 minutes.

Preheat the oven to 375°F/190°C. Line 2 baking sheets with baking parchment.

Unwrap the dough and roll out between 2 sheets of baking paper. Stamp out cookies with a 2½-inch/6-cm fluted round cutter and put them on the prepared baking sheets spaced well apart.

Bake for 10–15 minutes, until light golden brown. Let stand to cool on the baking sheets for 5–10 minutes, then using a palette knife, carefully transfer to wire racks to cool completely.

Remove the ice cream from the freezer about 15 minutes before serving to let it soften. Put a generous scoop of ice cream on half the cookies and top with the remaining cookies. Press together gently so that the filling spreads to the edges. If not serving immediately, wrap the cookies individually in plastic wrap and store in the freezer.

Keep me dry

This chapter focuses on all-important pantry ingredients—the sauces and condiments that add sparkle to cooking, zesty spices, canned fish, olives, oil and vinegar, syrups that add sweetness and gloss, and dependable standbys such as pasta, rice, and beans.

All these goodies can be bought in advance, and many of them stored for weeks or even months until you need them. However, a well-stocked pantry doesn't have to be overflowing. It's far better to have just a few items that get used up and replaced, rather than a vast stash of half-empty jars and bottles that have outstayed their welcome. It also pays to have a well-organized pantry, so you won't be rummaging for a mislaid ingredient when you're in the middle of cooking. It's a good idea to decant dry goods into airtight (and pest-proof) containers, away from light, heat, and moisture. Add labels so you can easily identify the contents. Check the expiration dates often, and chuck out anything that's past its best.

The chapter also includes apples, onions, and potatoes. These should be kept in a dry, cool, airy place, rather than the refrigerator—a well-ventilated wicker drawer or vegetable rack is ideal. Keep potatoes away from light, and remove any plastic packaging because it can encourage mold.

22. Bread

serves 4

1 red bell pepper, cored, seeded, and chopped

2 lb 4 oz/1 kg ripe tomatoes, cored and chopped

2 tbsp finely chopped onion

3 garlic cloves, crushed

1 cucumber, peeled and chopped

3½ slices stale bread, crumbled

3 tbsp red wine vinegar or sherry vinegar

3½ tbsp olive oil, plus extra for drizzling

ice cubes (optional)

salt and pepper

Gazpacho

Set aside a handful of the red bell pepper, a handful of the tomatoes, and half the chopped onion in the refrigerator. Put the rest in a food processor with the garlic and cucumber and puree until smooth. Add the bread, vinegar, and oil and blend again.

Season with salt and pepper to taste. If the soup is too thick, add some ice, then place in the refrigerator for 2 hours.

When ready to serve, check the vinegar and seasoning and ladle into bowls. Scatter over the reserved red pepper, tomatoes, and onions, then drizzle over a swirl of olive oil. Serve.

serves 2

2 tbsp margarine, softened

4 slices rye bread

2 tbsp thousand island dressing

4–6 oz/115–175 g cooked salt beef, thinly sliced

7 oz/200 g store-bought sauerkraut, drained

1 cup grated Gruyère cheese

vegetable oil, for frying

pickled gherkins, to serve

Reuben sandwich

Spread the margarine on one side of each slice of bread and lay margarine side down. Spread the other sides with 1 tablespoon of the dressing.

Divide the salt beef between 2 slices of the bread, tucking in the sides to fit. Divide the sauerkraut and make an even layer on top of the salt beef, before covering with the grated cheese. Top with the remaining slices of bread, margarine side facing up, and press firmly to compress the layers.

Heat a nonstick grill pan over medium–high heat and carefully slide the sandwiches into the pan. Using a spatula, press down on the tops of the sandwiches. Cook for 3 minutes, or until the undersides are crisp and golden. Carefully turn over the sandwiches, press down again, and cook for an additional 2 minutes, or until golden, the cheese is melted, and the salt beef is hot. Remove from the heat and transfer the sandwiches to a cutting board. Cut in half and serve with pickled gherkins.

3

serves 4–6

8 slices stale bread (about 9 oz/250 g)

4 large, ripe tomatoes

5–6 tbsp extra virgin olive oil

4 red, yellow, and/or orange bell peppers

½ cucumber

1 large red onion, finely chopped

8 canned anchovy fillets, drained and chopped

2 tbsp capers in brine, rinsed and patted dry about

4 tbsp red wine vinegar

2–3 tbsp balsamic vinegar

salt and pepper

fresh basil leaves, to garnish

Panzanella

Cut the bread into 1-inch/2.5-cm cubes and place in a large bowl. Quarter the tomatoes; reserve the juices. Using a teaspoon, scoop out the cores and seeds and discard, then finely chop the flesh. Add to the bread cubes.

Drizzle 5 tablespoons of the olive oil over the mixture and toss with your hands until well coated. Pour in the reserved tomato juice and toss again. Set aside for about 30 minutes. Meanwhile, cut the bell peppers in half and remove the cores and seeds. Place on a metal rack under a preheated hot broiler and broil for 10 minutes, or until the skins are charred and the flesh softened.

Place in a plastic bag, seal, and set aside for 20 minutes to allow the steam to loosen the skins. Remove the skins, then finely chop. Cut the cucumber in half lengthwise, then cut each half into 3 strips lengthwise. Using a teaspoon, scoop out and discard the seeds. Dice the cucumber.

Add the onion, peppers, cucumber, anchovy fillets, and capers to the bread and toss together. Sprinkle with the red wine vinegar and 2 tablespoons of the balsamic vinegar and season with salt and pepper.

Drizzle with extra olive oil or balsamic vinegar, if necessary. Sprinkle the fresh basil leaves over the salad and serve immediately.

4

serves 4–6

6 tbsp butter, softened

6 slices of thick white bread

⅓ cup mixed fruit

2 tbsp candied peel

3 large eggs

1¼ cups milk

⅔ cup heavy cream

¼ cup superfine sugar

whole nutmeg, for grating

1 tbsp raw sugar

cream, to serve

Bread & butter pudding

Preheat the oven to 350°F/180°C.

Use a little of the butter to grease an 8 x 10-inch/20 x 25-cm baking dish. Butter the slices of bread, cut into quarters, and arrange half overlapping in the dish.

Scatter half the fruit and peel over the bread, cover with the remaining bread slices, and add the remaining fruit and peel.

In a small mixing bowl, whisk the eggs well and mix in the milk, cream, and sugar. Pour this over the dessert and let stand for 15 minutes to let the bread to soak up some of the egg mixture. Tuck in most of the fruit so it doesn't burn in the oven. Grate the nutmeg over the top of the dessert, according to taste, and sprinkle over the raw sugar.

Place the dessert on a baking sheet and bake at the top of the oven for 30–40 minutes, until just set and golden brown.

Remove from the oven and serve warm with a little cream.

23. Pasta

serves 4

1 lb 10 oz/750 g mussels, scrubbed and debearded

2 tbsp olive oil

½ cup butter

4 slices lean bacon, chopped

1 onion, chopped

2 garlic cloves, finely chopped

scant ½ cup all-purpose flour

3 potatoes, thinly sliced

4 oz/115 g dried farfalle (pasta bows)

1¼ cups heavy cream

1 tbsp lemon juice

2 egg yolks

salt and pepper

2 tbsp finely chopped fresh parsley, to garnish

Mussel & pasta soup

Discard any mussels with broken shells or any that refuse to close when tapped. Bring a large, heavy-bottom pan of water to a boil. Add the mussels and olive oil and season to taste with pepper. Cover tightly and cook over high heat for 5 minutes, or until the mussels have opened. Remove the mussels with a slotted spoon, discarding any that remain closed. Strain the cooking liquid and set aside 5 cups.

Melt the butter in a clean pan. Add the bacon, onion, and garlic, and cook over low heat, stirring occasionally, for 5 minutes. Stir in the flour and cook, stirring, for 1 minute. Gradually stir in all but 2 tablespoons of the reserved cooking liquid and bring to a boil, stirring constantly. Add the potato slices and simmer for 5 minutes. Add the pasta and simmer for an additional 10 minutes.

Stir in the cream and lemon juice and season to taste with salt and pepper. Add the mussels. Mix the egg yolks and the remaining mussel cooking liquid together, then stir the mixture into the soup and cook for 4 minutes, until thickened.

Ladle the soup into warmed soup bowls, garnish with chopped parsley, and serve immediately.

serves 4

12 oz/350 g dried macaroni

6 tbsp butter, plus extra for greasing

2 small fennel bulbs, thinly sliced

2½ cups thinly sliced mushrooms

6 oz/175 g cooked, peeled shrimp

pinch of cayenne pepper

1¼ store-bought béchamel sauce

½ cup freshly grated Parmesan cheese

2 large tomatoes, halved and sliced

olive oil, for brushing

1 tsp dried oregano

salt

Macaroni & seafood casserole

Preheat the oven to 350°F/180°C. Grease a large ovenproof dish with butter. Bring a large pan of lightly salted water to a boil. Add the pasta, return to a boil, and cook for 8–10 minutes, or according to the package instructions. Drain and return to the pan. Add 2 tablespoons of the butter to the pasta, cover, shake the pan, and keep warm.

Melt the remaining butter in a separate pan. Add the fennel and cook for 3–4 minutes. Stir in the mushrooms and cook for an additional 2 minutes. Stir in the shrimp, then remove the pan from the heat.

Stir the cooked pasta, cayenne pepper, and the shrimp mixture into the béchamel sauce.

Pour the mixture into the greased ovenproof dish and spread evenly. Sprinkle over the Parmesan cheese and arrange the tomato slices in a ring around the edge. Brush the tomatoes with olive oil, then sprinkle over the oregano. Bake in the preheated oven for 25 minutes, or until golden brown. Serve immediately.

3

serves 4

1 lb/450 g asparagus tips
1 tbsp olive oil
8 oz/225 g Gorgonzola cheese, crumbled
¾ cup heavy cream
2 oz/350 g dried penne (pasta quills)
salt and pepper

Penne with asparagus & gorgonzola

Preheat the oven to 450°F/230°C. Place the asparagus tips in a single layer in a shallow ovenproof dish. Sprinkle with the oil and season to taste with salt and pepper. Turn to coat in the oil and seasoning. Roast in the preheated oven for 10–12 minutes, or until slightly browned and just tender. Set aside and keep warm.

Combine the crumbled cheese with the cream in a bowl. Season to taste with salt and pepper.

Bring a large saucepan of lightly salted water to a boil. Add the pasta, bring back to a boil, and cook for 8–10 minutes, or according to the package instructions. Drain and transfer to a warmed serving dish. Immediately add the asparagus and the cheese mixture. Toss well until the cheese has melted and the pasta is coated with the sauce. Serve immediately.

4

serves 4

3 tbsp olive oil

1 onion, chopped

1 red bell pepper, seeded and diced

1 orange bell pepper, seeded and diced

1 lb 12 oz/800 g canned chopped tomatoes

1 tbsp sun-dried tomato paste

1 tsp paprika

8 oz/225 g pepperoni sausage, sliced

2 tbsp chopped fresh flat-leaf parsley, plus extra to garnish

2 oz/350 g dried penne (pasta quills)

salt and pepper

Pepperoni & bell pepper pasta

Heat 2 tablespoons of the olive oil in a large, heavy-bottom skillet. Add the onion and cook over low heat, stirring occasionally, for 5 minutes, or until softened. Add the red and orange bell peppers, tomatoes and their can juices, sun-dried tomato paste, and paprika and bring to a boil.

Add the pepperoni and parsley and season to taste with salt and pepper. Stir well, bring to a boil, then reduce the heat and simmer for 10–15 minutes.

Meanwhile, bring a large, heavy-bottom pan of lightly salted water to a boil. Add the pasta, return to a boil, and cook for 8–10 minutes, or according to the package instructions. Drain well and transfer to a warmed serving dish. Add the remaining olive oil and toss. Add the sauce and toss again. Sprinkle with parsley and serve immediately.

24. Rice

serves 4

¼ cup long-grain white rice

3¼ cups chopped, cooked leftover turkey

1 small cooking apple, peeled, cored, and grated

1 small onion, finely chopped

1 garlic clove, finely chopped

1 tsp ground sage

½ tsp dried thyme

½ tsp ground allspice

vegetable oil, for frying

salt and pepper

Homemade turkey burgers

Cook the rice in a large pan of boiling salted water for about 10 minutes, or until tender. Drain, rinse under cold running water, then drain well again.

Put the cooked rice and all the remaining ingredients in a large bowl and mix well together. Season with salt and pepper.

With wet hands, shape the mixture into 8 thick burgers. Pour a little oil into a large, nonstick skillet, add the burgers, and cook for about 10 minutes, turning them over several times, until they are golden brown. Remove from the skillet and serve while hot.

serves 4

2 tbsp vegetable oil or peanut oil

2 garlic cloves, finely chopped

2 fresh red chiles, seeded and chopped

2 cups sliced button mushrooms

1¾ cup snow peas, halved

6–8 baby corn, halved

3 tbsp soy sauce

1 tbsp light brown sugar

a few basil leaves

3 cups long-grain white rice, cooked and cooled

2 eggs, beaten

crispy, fried onions (optional)

Egg-fried rice with vegetables

Heat the oil in a wok or large skillet and sauté the garlic and chiles for 2–3 minutes.

Add the mushrooms, snow peas, and corn, and stir-fry for 2–3 minutes before adding the soy sauce, sugar, and basil. Stir in the rice.

Push the mixture to one side of the wok and add the eggs to the bottom. Stir until lightly set before combining into the rice mixture.

Transfer to serving plates and top with the crispy, fried onions, if using.

serves 6

2 cups long-grain white rice
2–3 shallots, finely chopped
1 cup fresh mint leaves, finely chopped
soy sauce, to serve

chicken stock

8 cups water
1 chicken, about 2–2½ lb/900 g–1.1 kg
2-inch/5-cm piece fresh ginger, peeled and
   thinly sliced
4 scallions, trimmed and crushed
2 to 3 tbsp fish sauce

Chicken, mint & shallot rice

For the stock, put the water and chicken in a large saucepan and bring to a boil over high heat. Reduce the heat to medium–low and add the ginger, scallions, and fish sauce. Simmer for 1½ hours, or until reduced by about half, skimming off any foam.

Transfer the cooked chicken to a platter and separate the meat from the bones and skin. Shred the meat and set aside. Strain the stock, discarding the solids, and remove any fat.

Put the rice in a bowl and cover with cold water. Swirl the rice to loosen any starch and drain. Repeat twice more until the water runs just clear. Transfer the rice to a large saucepan and add 2¾ cups of the stock. Cover and bring to a boil over high heat. Reduce the heat to medium–low and cook for 20 to 25 minutes, or until the stock is fully absorbed. Let rest for 10 minutes, then fluff up the rice with a fork.

Add the shallots, mint, and chicken to the rice and mix well. Serve in individual bowls, and serve with the soy sauce.

4

serves 4

½ cup long-grain rice

4 scallions

8 oz/225 g canned pineapple chunks in
    natural juice

1 cup canned corn, drained

2 red bell peppers, seeded and diced

3 tbsp golden raisins

salt and pepper

dressing

1 tbsp peanut oil

1 tbsp hazelnut oil

1 tbsp light soy sauce

1 garlic clove, finely chopped

1 tsp chopped fresh ginger

Tropical rice salad

Cook the rice in a large pan of lightly salted boiling water for 15 minutes,
or until tender. Drain thoroughly and rinse under cold running water.
Place the rice in a large serving bowl.

Using a sharp knife, finely chop the scallions. Drain the pineapple
chunks, reserving the juice in a measuring cup. Add the pineapple
chunks, corn, red bell peppers, chopped scallions, and golden raisins
to the rice and mix lightly.

Add all the dressing ingredients to the reserved pineapple juice, whisking
well, and season to taste with salt and pepper. Pour the dressing over the
salad and toss until the salad is thoroughly coated. Serve immediately.

25. Noodles

serves 4–6

1 lb 2 oz/500 g dried egg noodles
1 tbsp corn oil
4 skinless, boneless chicken thighs, diced
1 bunch of scallions, sliced
2 garlic cloves, chopped
¾-inch/2-cm piece fresh ginger, finely
    chopped
3¾ cups chicken stock
¾ cup coconut milk
3 tsp red curry paste
3 tbsp peanut butter
2 tbsp light soy sauce
1 small red bell pepper, seeded and
    chopped
½ cup frozen peas
salt and pepper

Chicken noodle soup

Place the noodles in a large saucepan of boiling water, then
immediately remove from the heat. Cover and let the noodles rest for
6 minutes, stirring once halfway through the time.

Meanwhile, heat the oil in a preheated wok. Add the chicken and
stir-fry for 5 minutes, or until lightly browned. Add the white part of
the scallions, the garlic, and ginger and stir-fry for 2 minutes.

Add the stock, coconut milk, curry paste, peanut butter, and soy
sauce. Season to taste with salt and pepper. Bring to a boil, stirring
constantly, then simmer for 8 minutes, stirring occasionally. Add the
bell pepper, peas, and green scallion tops and cook for an additional
2 minutes.

Drain the noodles, then add them to the wok and heat through.
Spoon into warmed serving bowls and serve immediately.

serves 4

1 lb 2 oz/500 g dried egg noodles
3 tbsp sunflower oil
2 tbsp sesame oil
1 garlic clove, crushed
1 tbsp smooth peanut butter
1 small green chile, seeded and very
    finely chopped
3 tbsp toasted sesame seeds
1 tbsp light soy sauce
½ tbsp lime juice
salt and pepper
4 tbsp chopped fresh cilantro

Hot sesame noodles

Place the noodles in a large saucepan of boiling water, then immediately
remove from the heat. Cover and let the noodles stand for 6 minutes,
stirring once halfway through the time.

Meanwhile, make the dressing. Mix together the sunflower oil, sesame oil,
crushed garlic, and peanut butter in a mixing bowl until smooth.

Add the chopped green chile, sesame seeds, and light soy sauce to the
other dressing ingredients. Add the lime juice, according to taste, and
mix well. Season with salt and pepper.

Drain the noodles thoroughly, then place in a warmed serving bowl.

Add the dressing and chopped fresh cilantro to the noodles and toss well
to mix. Serve hot as a main course or as an accompaniment.

3

serves 4

2 tbsp peanut or vegetable oil

1 bunch of scallions, coarsely chopped

1-inch/2.5-cm piece fresh ginger, finely chopped

2 lemongrass stalks, halved

2 carrots, cut into thin sticks

1 small head broccoli, cut into florets

6–8 baby corn, halved lengthwise

10 canned water chestnuts, drained

1 tbsp red curry paste

8 oz/225 g dried egg noodles

4 tbsp sesame seeds

salt

Vegetable stir-fry

Heat the oil in a preheated wok. Add the scallions, ginger, and lemongrass and stir-fry over medium–high heat for 2–3 minutes, or until starting to soften. Add the carrots, broccoli, and baby corn and stir-fry for 3–4 minutes, until starting to soften. Add the water chestnuts and curry paste and stir well, then stir-fry for an additional 2–3 minutes. Discard the lemongrass.

Place the noodles in a large saucepan of boiling water, then immediately remove from the heat. Cover and let the noodles rest for 6 minutes, stirring once halfway through the time.

Add the noodles to the stir-fried vegetables and serve immediately.

serves 2

1 tbsp red curry paste

2 tbsp soy sauce

12 oz/350 g pork tenderloin, trimmed

8 oz/225 g dried egg noodles

2 tbsp peanut or vegetable oil

1 red onion, chopped

1-inch/2.5-cm piece fresh ginger,
   finely chopped

1 garlic clove, finely chopped

1 orange bell pepper, seeded
   and chopped

1 red bell pepper, seeded and chopped

1 tbsp black pepper

1 small bunch of fresh chives, snipped

handful of fresh cilantro, chopped

Pork with peppered noodles

Mix the curry paste and soy sauce together in a small bowl and spread over the pork tenderloin. Cover and let marinate in the refrigerator for 1 hour.

Preheat the oven to 400°F/200°C. Roast the pork in the preheated oven for 20–25 minutes, or until cooked through. Remove from the oven, then cover with foil and let rest for 15 minutes.

Place the noodles in a large saucepan of boiling water, then immediately remove from the heat. Cover and let the noodles rest for 6 minutes, stirring once halfway through the time.

Heat the oil in a preheated wok. Add the onion, ginger, and garlic and stir-fry over medium–high heat for 1–2 minutes. Add the orange and red bell peppers and black pepper, and stir-fry for 2–3 minutes, or until tender. Stir in the chives and most of the cilantro.

Add the drained noodles to the bell pepper mixture and toss together until well mixed. Divide between 2 serving dishes. Slice the pork and arrange on top of the noodles. Sprinkle with the remaining cilantro and serve immediately.

3

serves 4

2 tbsp French green lentils
1 bay leaf
2 scallions, finely chopped
scant ¼ cup diced red bell pepper
1 tbsp chopped fresh parsley
8 cherry tomatoes, halved
⅓ cup arugula
1 oz/25 g goat cheese, sliced or crumbled

dressing

1 tsp olive oil
1 tsp balsamic vinegar
½ tsp honey
1 garlic clove, crushed or finely chopped

Lentil & goat cheese salad

Rinse the lentils and put in a medium pan. Add the bay leaf and cover with plenty of cold water. Bring to a boil, then reduce the heat and simmer for 20–30 minutes, or until the lentils are tender.

Drain the lentils and transfer to a bowl. Add the scallions, bell pepper, parsley, and cherry tomatoes. Mix well.

To make the dressing, whisk together the oil, vinegar, honey, and garlic and stir into the lentils. Serve on a bed of arugula, sprinkled with the goat cheese.

serves 4–6

2 tbsp olive oil

1 large onion, finely chopped

1 large garlic clove, crushed

½ tbsp ground cumin

½ tsp ground ginger

1 heaping cup French green lentils

2½ cups vegetable stock

4 cups young spinach leaves

2 tbsp fresh mint leaves

1 tbsp fresh cilantro leaves

1 tbsp fresh flat-leaf parsley leaves

freshly squeezed lemon juice

salt and pepper

strips of lemon zest, to garnish

Spiced lentils with spinach

Heat the oil in a large skillet over medium heat. Add the onion and cook, stirring occasionally, for about 6 minutes. Stir in the garlic, cumin, and ginger and cook, stirring occasionally, until the onion starts to brown.

Stir in the lentils. Pour in enough stock to cover the lentils by 1 inch/2.5 cm and bring to a boil. Lower the heat and simmer for 20–30 minutes, until the lentils are tender.

Meanwhile, rinse the spinach leaves in several changes of cold water and shake dry. Finely chop the mint, cilantro leaves, and parsley.

If there isn't any stock left in the skillet, add a little extra. Add the spinach and stir through until it just wilts. Stir in the mint, cilantro, and parsley. Adjust the seasoning, adding lemon juice and salt and pepper. Transfer to a serving bowl and serve, garnished with lemon zest.

27. Extra Virgin Olive Oil

serves 4

1 lb/450 g firm porcini
generous ⅓ cup extra virgin olive oil
2 garlic cloves, finely chopped
large handful of parsley, chopped
salt and pepper
sourdough toast, to serve

serves 4

1 lb/450 g dried spaghetti
½ cup extra virgin olive oil
3 garlic cloves, finely chopped
3 tbsp chopped fresh flat-leaf parsley
salt and pepper

Porcini with parsley & extra virgin olive oil

Clean the porcini and separate the heads from the stalks. Chop the stalks roughly and set aside. Place a skillet over high heat and add the oil. When it's shimmering, add the porcini heads and fry. Check the undersides—when they have begun to brown, turn them over. Season with salt and pepper.

Add the garlic, chopped porcini stalks, and parsley and sauté for 5–10 minutes, until the flavors really start to release and the garlic's bite eases a little.

Serve on slices of sourdough toast with a drizzle of the hot olive oil from the pan.

Spaghetti olio e aglio

Bring a large, heavy-bottom pan of lightly salted water to a boil. Add the pasta, return to a boil, and cook for 8–10 minutes, or according to the package instructions.

Meanwhile, heat the olive oil in a heavy-bottom skillet. Add the garlic and a pinch of salt and cook over low heat, stirring constantly, for 3–4 minutes, or until golden. Do not let the garlic brown or it will taste bitter. Remove the skillet from the heat.

Drain the pasta and transfer to a large, warmed serving dish. Pour in the garlic-flavored olive oil, then add the chopped parsley and season to taste with salt and pepper. Toss well and serve immediately.

3

serves 4

3 large garlic cloves, finely chopped

2 egg yolks

1 cup extra virgin olive oil

1 tbsp lemon juice

1 tbsp lime juice

1 tbsp Dijon mustard

1 tbsp chopped fresh tarragon

salt and pepper

Aïoli

Ensure that all the ingredients are at room temperature. Place the garlic and egg yolks in a food processor and process until well blended. With the motor running, pour in the oil, teaspoon by teaspoon, through the feeder tube until the mixture starts to thicken, then pour in the remaining oil in a thin stream until a thick mayonnaise forms.

Add the lemon and lime juices, mustard, and tarragon and season to taste with salt and pepper. Blend until smooth, then transfer to a nonmetallic bowl.

Cover with plastic wrap and chill until required.

4

makes about 1 cup

2¼ cups fresh basil leaves

1 garlic clove

2 tbsp toasted pine nuts

6 tbsp extra virgin olive oil

2 tbsp freshly grated Parmesan cheese

1–2 tsp freshly squeezed lemon juice (optional)

salt and pepper

Pesto

Tear the basil leaves coarsely into pieces and put in a large mortar with the garlic, pine nuts, and 1 tablespoon of the oil. Pound with a pestle to form a paste.

Gradually work in the remaining oil to form a thick sauce. Add salt and pepper to taste and stir in the Parmesan cheese. If liked, thin slightly with the lemon juice.

Alternatively, put the basil leaves with the pine nuts and a little of the oil in a food processor and process for 1 minute. Scrape down the sides of the bowl. With the motor running, gradually add the remaining oil in a thin, steady stream.

Scrape into a bowl, then stir in pepper to taste and the Parmesan cheese. If liked, thin with the lemon juice.

Keep me dry 129

20. Balsamic Vinegar

serves 2

about 16 cherry tomatoes

4 garlic cloves, unpeeled

1 tbsp olive oil

7 oz/200 g soft rind goat cheese, such as Pyramid

2 cups arugula

2 tbsp balsamic vinegar

salt and pepper

a few fresh basil leaves, to garnish

serves 2–4

10 sprigs of rosemary, 2 inches/ 5 cm long

4 cloves garlic

1 cup balsamic vinegar

Goat cheese salad with balsamic vinegar

Preheat the oven to 350°F/180°C. Put the tomatoes and garlic in a small roasting pan. Sprinkle them with the oil and season well with salt and pepper. Cook at the top of the preheated oven for 20 minutes.

Remove the top and bottom rinds from the goat cheese and cut in half horizontally. If you are using two smaller cheeses, cut them both in half horizontally.

Place the cheese pieces in a heatproof dish and cook under a hot broiler for 3–4 minutes, until they begin to melt and turn golden.

Arrange the arugula on two plates. Remove the tomatoes and garlic from the oven, using a slotted spoon, and reserve the roasting juices. Arrange the tomatoes and garlic around the plates and put the cheese in the center.

Add the balsamic vinegar to the juices in the roasting pan and mix well to make a dressing. Drizzle the dressing over the cheese and salad and serve garnished with the basil leaves.

Rosemary & garlic balsamic vinegar

Wash the rosemary sprigs, dry, and tear off the leaves from the stems. Split the garlic cloves in half lengthwise. Combine the leaves and garlic halves in a clean jar.

In a saucepan over medium heat, heat the balsamic vinegar until it just starts to bubble around the edges of the pan. Wait until it cools a little, then pour into the jar with the rosemary and garlic. When it is completely cool, cover the jar and store in a cool, dark place. Check occasionally to see if the vinegar has reached the desired strength.

Before using, strain the vinegar through a fine strainer or cheesecloth into a clean jar. Add a fresh sprig of rosemary for decoration, cover again, and store in a cool, dark place.

Keep me dry

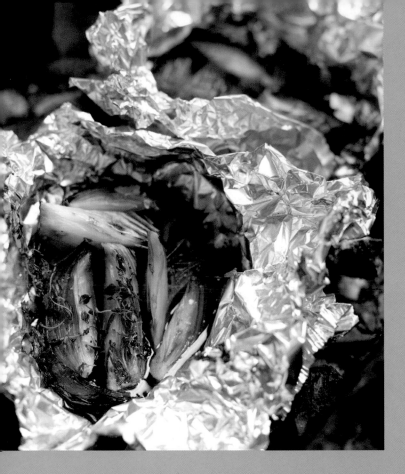

3

serves 4

4 red onions, peeled and cut into chunky
  wedges

4 tsp honey

4 tbsp balsamic vinegar

1 tsp fresh thyme, finely chopped

salt and pepper

Roasted balsamic & honey onions

Preheat the broiler to high. Divide the onion wedges between 4 squares
of double-thickness foil. Bring up the sides of the foil a little.

Drizzle the honey and balsamic vinegar over the onions, add the
thyme, and season with salt and pepper. Loosely seal the packages and
place under the broiler for 15–20 minutes, or until the onions are tender.

4

serves 4

1 tsp honey

⅓ cup water

1 lb/450 g ripe strawberries, hulled

2 tbsp balsamic vinegar

4 baby strawberries or wild strawberries,
   halved, to decorate (optional)

fresh mint sprigs, to decorate (optional)

Strawberry & balsamic vinegar semifreddo

Set the freezer to its coldest setting at least 2 hours before freezing. Pour the honey and water into a pan and bring to a boil, stirring occasionally. Reduce the heat then add the strawberries and simmer for 2 minutes. Remove from the heat and let cool.

Place the strawberries and syrup in a food processor with the balsamic vinegar and process for 30 seconds, or until a chunky mixture is formed.

Pour the mixture into a freezerproof container and freeze for 1–1½ hours, or until semifrozen. Stir at least once during freezing. Scoop spoonfuls of the semifreddo into glasses, and serve decorated with baby strawberries or wild strawberries, and mint sprigs, if using. Remember to return the freezer to its original setting afterward.

29. Soy Sauce

serves 4

2 fresh red chiles, seeded
  and coarsely chopped

6 tbsp rice vinegar

5 cups vegetable stock

2 lemongrass stalks, halved

4 tbsp soy sauce

1 tbsp light brown sugar or jaggery

juice of ½ lime

2 tbsp peanut or vegetable oil

8 oz/225 g firm tofu (drained weight), cut
  into ½-inch/1-cm cubes

14 oz/400 g canned straw mushrooms,
  drained

4 scallions, chopped

1 small head bok choy, shredded

Hot & sour soup

Mix the chiles and vinegar together in a nonmetallic bowl. Cover and
let stand at room temperature for 1 hour.

Meanwhile, bring the stock to a boil in a pan. Add the lemongrass,
soy sauce, sugar, and lime juice, then reduce the heat and simmer
for 20–30 minutes.

Heat the oil in a preheated wok, then add the tofu cubes and stir-fry
over high heat for 2–3 minutes, or until browned all over. (You may
need to do this in 2 batches, depending on the size of the wok.)
Remove with a slotted spoon and drain on paper towels.

Add the chiles and vinegar with the tofu, mushrooms, and half the
scallions to the stock mixture and cook for 10 minutes. Mix the
remaining scallions with the bok choy and sprinkle over the soup
before serving.

serves 4

9 oz/250 g medium egg noodles

2 tbsp sunflower oil

2 cups shredded, cooked chicken
  breasts

1 garlic clove, finely chopped

1 red bell pepper, seeded and thinly
  sliced

3½ oz/100 g shiitake mushrooms,
  sliced

6 scallions, sliced

1 cup bean sprouts

3 tbsp soy sauce

1 tbsp sesame oil

Chicken chow mein

Place the egg noodles in a large bowl or dish and break them up slightly.
Pour enough boiling water over the noodles to cover and leave to stand
while preparing the other ingredients.

Heat the sunflower oil in a large preheated wok. Add the chicken, garlic,
bell pepper, mushrooms, scallions, and beansprouts to the wok and stir-
fry for about 5 minutes.

Drain the noodles thoroughly. Add the noodles to the wok, toss well, and
stir-fry for an additional 5 minutes.

Drizzle the soy sauce and sesame oil over the chow mein and toss until
well combined. Transfer to warmed serving bowls and serve immediately.

3

serves 4

1 lb 2 oz/500 g sweet potatoes

2 garlic cloves, crushed

1 small fresh green chile, seeded and chopped

2 fresh cilantro sprigs, chopped

1 tbsp dark soy sauce

all-purpose flour, for coating

vegetable oil, for frying

sesame seeds, for sprinkling

soy-tomato sauce

2 tsp vegetable oil

1 garlic clove, finely chopped

1½ tsp finely chopped fresh ginger

3 tomatoes, skinned and chopped

2 tbsp dark soy sauce

1 tbsp lime juice

2 tbsp chopped fresh cilantro

Sweet potato cakes with soy-tomato sauce

To make the soy-tomato sauce, heat the oil in a wok and stir-fry the garlic and ginger over a medium heat for about 1 minute. Add the tomatoes and stir-fry for an additional 2 minutes. Remove the wok from the heat and stir in the soy sauce, lime juice, and chopped cilantro. Reserve and keep warm.

Peel the sweet potatoes and grate finely—you can do this quickly with a food processor. Place the garlic, chile, and cilantro in a mortar and crush to a smooth paste with a pestle. Stir in the soy sauce and mix with the sweet potatoes.

Put some flour on a plate. Divide the mixture into 12 equal portions, toss each portion in the flour until coated, and pat into a flat, round shape.

Heat a shallow layer of oil in a wide skillet over high heat. Fry the sweet potato patties, in batches, until golden, turning once.

Drain the sweet potato cakes on paper towels, transfer to a warm serving dish, sprinkle with sesame seeds, and serve hot with the soy-tomato sauce.

4

serves 4

9 oz/250 g package of tofu, drained and
   cubed
9 oz/250 g medium egg noodles
1 tbsp peanut or vegetable oil
1 red bell pepper, seeded and sliced
2 cups broccoli florets
18–20 baby corn, halved lengthwise
2 3 tbsp water
2 scallions, finely sliced
1 tbsp sesame seeds, toasted (optional)
salt

marinade

1 garlic clove, finely chopped
1-inch/2.5-cm piece fresh ginger, peeled
   and grated
1 tsp sesame oil
1 tbsp honey
2 tbsp dark soy sauce

Vegetables with Chinese noodles

Mix together the ingredients for the marinade in a shallow dish. Add the
tofu and spoon the marinade over. Refrigerate for 1 hour, turning the tofu
occasionally, to let the flavors steep.

Preheat the oven to 400°F/200°C. Using a slotted spoon, remove the tofu
from the marinade and reserve the liquid. Arrange the tofu on a baking
sheet and roast for 20 minutes, turning occasionally, until the tofu pieces
are golden and crisp on all sides.

Meanwhile, cook the noodles in plenty of salted boiling water according
to the package instructions, until the noodles are tender, then drain.
Rinse the noodles under cold running water and drain again.

Heat a wok or heavy-bottom skillet, then add the oil. Add the bell pepper,
broccoli, and corn and stir-fry, tossing and stirring continuously, over a
medium–high heat for 5–8 minutes, or until the vegetables have softened.
Add the water and continue to stir-fry until the vegetables are just tender
but remain slightly crunchy.

Stir in the marinade, noodles, tofu, and scallions and stir-fry until heated
through. Serve sprinkled with sesame seeds, if using.

30. Red Wine

serves 4–6

about 5 tbsp canola oil or sunflower oil

4 lb 8 oz/2 kg bone-in beef short ribs, cut
into 4-inch/10-cm pieces

1 large onion, chopped

1 large carrot, peeled and chopped

1 celery stalk, chopped

1 bottle red wine

4½ cups beef stock

1 bouquet garni

4 tbsp butter

1 lb 9 oz/700 g mushrooms, sliced

1 tbsp fresh thyme leaves,
or ½ tbsp dried thyme leaves

salt and pepper

Red wine-braised beef

Preheat the oven to 325°F/160°C. Heat 4 tablespoons of oil in a large
casserole over medium–high heat. Brown the ribs on all sides in
batches, adding more oil if necessary, and set aside. Add the onion,
carrot, and celery and fry for 5 minutes, until tender. Spoon off any
excess fat. Pour in the wine and stock and bring to a boil.

Reduce the heat and return the ribs to the casserole with the
bouquet garni, salt and pepper to taste, and enough water to cover.
Scrunch a piece of foil on top, cover, and return to a boil. Put in the
preheated oven for 1½ hours, or until the ribs are just tender.
Do not overcook.

Skim the copious amount of fat from the surface, remove the ribs,
and strain the liquid. Return the ribs and liquid to the casserole and
set aside.

Melt the butter with the remaining oil in a large skillet. Add the
mushrooms and stir for 2 minutes. Add the thyme and salt and
pepper to taste, then stir for an additional 3 minutes, or until the
mushrooms release their liquid.

Stir the mushrooms into the casserole. Place over medium–high heat
and let bubble slightly, uncovered, for 45 minutes, until the sauce is
reduced and thick. Remove any loose bones. Adjust the seasoning
and serve.

serves 4

4 duck portions, about 5½ oz/150 g
each

1 red onion, cut into wedges

2–3 garlic cloves, chopped

1 large carrot, chopped

2 tbsp all-purpose flour

1¼ cups red wine

⅞ cup stock or water

3-inch/7.5-cm strip of orange rind

2 tsp red currant jelly

4 oz/115 g sugar snap peas

1–2 tsp olive oil

4 oz/115 g white mushrooms

Duck & red wine casserole

Remove and discard the fat from the duck. Lightly rinse and pat dry with
paper towels.

Heat a large, deep skillet for 1 minute, until warm but not piping hot. Put
the duck portions in the skillet and heat gently until the fat starts to run.
Increase the heat a little, then cook, turning over halfway through, for
5 minutes, or until browned on both sides and sealed. Using a slotted
spoon, transfer the duck portions to a flameproof casserole.

Add 1 tablespoon of the duck fat to the skillet and cook the onion, garlic,
and carrot, stirring frequently, for 5 minutes, or until softened. Sprinkle
in the flour and cook, stirring constantly, for 2 minutes, then remove the
skillet from the heat. Gradually stir in the wine and stock, then return to
the heat and bring to a boil, stirring. Add the orange rind and red currant
jelly. Pour over the duck portions in the casserole, cover, and simmer,
stirring occasionally, for 1–1¼ hours.

Cook the sugar snap peas in a pan of boiling water for 3 minutes, then
drain and add to the stew. Meanwhile heat the olive oil in a small pan and
cook the mushrooms, stirring frequently, for 3 minutes, or until beginning
to soften. Add to the stew. Cook the stew for an additional 5 minutes, or
until the duck is tender. Serve immediately.

3

serves 4

grated rind and juice of 1 orange

1¼ cups red wine

3 tbsp honey

1 cinnamon stick

1 vanilla bean

½ tsp apple pie spice

1 clove

4 firm, ripe pears

½ tsp arrowroot or potato flour

whipped cream, to serve (optional)

Pears in red wine sauce

Bring a pan of water to a boil. Meanwhile, put the orange rind and juice, wine, honey, cinnamon stick, vanilla bean, apple pie spice, and clove in a pan and bring to a boil, stirring frequently, then remove the pan from the heat.

Peel the pears, leaving the stem intact, and cut off a small slice from the bottom so that they will stand upright. Put them into a heatproof bowl and pour the wine mixture over them. Cover the bowl with a sheet of foil and tie in place with kitchen string.

Put the bowl into a steamer and cover with a tight-fitting lid. Set the steamer over the pan and steam for 35–40 minutes, until the pears are tender.

Remove the bowl from the steamer and let cool completely. Transfer the pears to a serving dish, standing them upright. Remove and discard the cinnamon stick, vanilla bean, and clove from the wine mixture and pour it into a small pan. Bring to a boil and cook until reduced to about ⅔ cup. Reduce the heat to a simmer.

Put the arrowroot or potato flour into a small bowl and stir in 2 tablespoons of the wine sauce to make a paste. Stir the paste into the pan and simmer gently, stirring constantly, for 2 minutes, until the sauce has thickened. Remove the pan from the heat and let cool.

Pour the wine sauce over the pears and chill in the refrigerator for at least 3 hours before serving with whipped cream, if you like.

4

makes about 1 lb 8 oz/675 g

1 lb/450 g tart cooking apples, washed
  and cut into chunks
2½ cups water
1 bottle red wine
3½ cups sugar (see method)

Wine jelly

Place the apples in a large pan together with the water and wine. Bring
to a boil, then reduce the heat and simmer for 30 minutes, or until the
apples are very soft and pulpy. Strain through a jelly bag.

Once all the juice has been extracted, measure, then return to the rinsed-
out pan. Add the sugar, allowing 2¼ cups of sugar for every 2½ cups
of juice. Heat gently, stirring frequently, until the sugar has completely
dissolved. Bring to a boil and boil rapidly for 15 minutes, or until the
setting point is reached.

Let cool slightly. Skim, then pot into warmed sterilized jars and cover the
tops with wax disks. When completely cold, cover with cellophane or lids,
then label and store in a cool place.

31. Vegetable Stock

serves 6

2 carrots, sliced

1 onion, diced

1 garlic clove, crushed

3 medium new potatoes, diced

2 celery sticks, sliced

14 oz/400 g canned chopped tomatoes

2½ cups vegetable stock

1 bay leaf

1 tsp dried mixed herbs

½ cup corn kernels, frozen or canned, drained

2–3 leaves green cabbage, shredded

pepper

Chunky vegetable soup

Put the carrots, onion, garlic, potatoes, celery, tomatoes and stock into a large saucepan. Stir in the bay leaf and herbs.

Add the corn kernels and cabbage and return to a boil. Reduce the heat, cover, and simmer for 5 minutes, or until the vegetables are tender. Remove and discard the bay leaf. Season to taste with pepper.

Ladle into warmed soup bowls and serve immediately.

serves 4

12 oz/350 g lean pork tenderloin

1 tbsp vegetable oil

1 medium onion, chopped

2 garlic cloves, crushed

2 tbsp all-purpose flour

2 tbsp tomato paste

generous 1¾ cups chicken or vegetable stock

1 cup sliced white mushrooms

1 large green bell pepper, seeded

½ tsp freshly grated nutmeg, plus extra to garnish

4 tbsp lowfat plain yogurt, plus extra to serve

salt and pepper

boiled rice with chopped fresh parsley, to serve

Pork stroganoff

Trim off any fat or gristle from the pork and cut into ½-inch/1-cm thick slices. Heat the vegetable oil in a large, heavy-bottom skillet and gently fry the pork, onion, and garlic for 4–5 minutes, or until lightly browned.

Stir in the flour and tomato paste, then pour in the chicken stock and stir to mix thoroughly. Add the mushrooms, bell pepper, salt and pepper to taste, and nutmeg. Bring to a boil, cover, and simmer for 20 minutes, or until the pork is tender and cooked through.

Remove the skillet from the heat and stir in the yogurt. Transfer the pork to 4 large, warmed serving plates and serve with boiled rice sprinkled with chopped fresh parsley and an extra spoonful of yogurt, garnished with freshly grated nutmeg.

3

serves 3–4

4 cups vegetable stock

5 tbsp butter

1 tbsp olive oil, plus extra for brushing

1 red onion, finely chopped

1 garlic clove, finely chopped

1½ cups risotto rice

⅔ cup dry white wine

9 oz/250 g frozen baby fava beans

3 large boneless duck breasts, about
1 lb/450 g in total

½ cup freshly grated Parmesan cheese

salt and pepper

Duck & fava bean risotto

Bring the stock to a boil in a saucepan, then reduce the heat and keep simmering gently over a low heat while you are cooking the risotto.

Meanwhile, heat the butter and the oil in a deep saucepan over a medium heat until the butter has melted. Add the onion and garlic and fry for about 5 minutes, until softened but not browned. Reduce the heat, add the rice, and mix to coat in oil and butter. Cook, stirring constantly, for 2–3 minutes, or until the grains are translucent. Add the wine and cook, stirring constantly, until it has reduced.

Gradually add the hot stock, a ladleful at a time. Stir constantly and add more liquid as the rice absorbs each addition. After about 15 minutes, stir in the fava beans. Cook for an additional 5 minutes, or until all the liquid has been absorbed and the rice is creamy but still firm to the bite.

Meanwhile, brush a grill pan or heavy-bottom skillet with oil and heat. Put the duck breasts on the griddle and cook over a medium heat for about 15 minutes, turning several times and ensuring that the skin is browned and crispy. Remove from the pan and slice thinly.

When the risotto is cooked, remove from the heat and stir in the duck and any juices, the Parmesan cheese and remaining butter. Season to taste with salt and pepper and serve immediately.

4

serves 4

1¼ cups dried cannellini beans

2 tbsp olive oil

4–8 pearl onions, halved

2 celery stalks, cut into ¼-inch/5-mm slices

16–18 baby-carrots, scrubbed and halved if large

2–3 medium–size new potatoes, scrubbed and halved, or cut into quarters if large

3¾–5 cups vegetable stock

1 fresh bouquet garni

1½–2 tbsp light soy sauce

8–10 baby corn

1 cup frozen or shelled fresh fava beans, thawed if frozen

½–1 savoy or spring (Primo) cabbage, about 8 oz/225 g

1½ tbsp cornstarch

2 tbsp cold water

salt and pepper

½ cup grated Parmesan or sharp cheddar cheese, to serve

Spring stew

Pick over the cannellini beans and rinse thoroughly, then drain and put in a large bowl. Cover with plenty of cold water and let soak overnight. The next day, drain, put in a pan, and cover with cold water. Bring to a boil and boil rapidly for 10 minutes, then drain and set aside.

Heat the oil in a large, heavy-bottom pan with a tight-fitting lid, and cook the vegetables, stirring frequently, for 5 minutes, or until softened. Add the stock, drained beans, bouquet garni, and soy sauce, then bring to a boil. Reduce the heat, then cover and simmer for 12 minutes.

Add the baby corn and fava beans and season to taste with salt and pepper. Simmer for an additional 3 minutes.

Meanwhile, discard the outer leaves and hard central core from the cabbage and shred the leaves. Add to the pan and simmer for an additional 3–5 minutes, or until all the vegetables are tender.

Blend the cornstarch with the water, then stir into the pan and cook, stirring, for 4–6 minutes, or until the liquid has thickened. Serve the cheese separately for stirring into the stew.

32. Chiles

serves 6

4 tbsp corn oil

2 onions, chopped

1 garlic clove, chopped

1 tbsp all-purpose flour

2 lb/900 g braising beef, diced

1¼ cups beef stock

1¼ cups red wine

2–3 fresh red chiles, seeded and chopped

1 lb 12 oz/800 g canned red kidney beans, drained and rinsed

14 oz/400 g canned chopped tomatoes

salt and pepper

tortilla chips, to serve

Chili con carne

Heat half of the oil in a heavy-bottom pan. Add half the chopped onions and the garlic and cook, stirring occasionally, for 5 minutes, until softened. Remove with a slotted spoon.

Place the flour on a plate and season well with salt and pepper, then toss the meat in the flour to coat. Cook the meat, in batches, until browned all over, then return all the meat and the onion mixture to the pan. Pour in the stock and wine and bring to a boil, stirring. Reduce the heat and let simmer for 1 hour.

Meanwhile, heat the remaining oil in a skillet. Add the remaining onion and the red chiles and cook, stirring occasionally, for 5 minutes. Add the beans and tomatoes with their juices and break up with a wooden spoon. Let simmer for 25 minutes, until thickened.

Divide the meat among individual plates, top with the bean mixture, and serve with tortilla chips.

serves 4

18–20 small new potatoes

⅔ cup vegetable oil

1 tsp chili powder

1 fresh green chile, seeded and finely chopped

½ tsp caraway seeds

1 tsp salt

basil leaves, shredded, to garnish

Chile roast potatoes

Preheat the oven to 400°F/200°C. Cook the potatoes in a saucepan of boiling water for 10 minutes, then drain thoroughly.

Pour a little of the oil into a shallow roasting pan to coat the bottom. Heat the oil in the preheated oven, for 10 minutes. Add the potatoes to the pan and brush them with the hot oil.

In a small bowl, mix together the chili powder, fresh chile, caraway seeds, and salt. Sprinkle the mixture over the potatoes, turning to coat them all over.

Add the remaining oil to the pan and roast in the oven for about 15 minutes, or until the potatoes are cooked through.

Using a slotted spoon, remove the potatoes from the the oil, draining them thoroughly, and transfer them to a warmed serving dish. Sprinkle the shredded basil over the top and serve immediately.

3

serves 4

2 tbsp corn oil
1 onion, chopped
1 garlic clove, finely chopped
1 tsp grated fresh ginger
1 tsp ground coriander
½ tsp chili powder
¼ tsp ground turmeric
1½ cups fresh ground lamb
7 oz/200 g canned chopped tomatoes
1 tbsp chopped fresh mint
scant ⅔ cup fresh or frozen peas
2 carrots, sliced into thin sticks
1 fresh green chile, seeded and finely
  chopped
1 tbsp chopped fresh cilantro
salt
fresh mint sprigs, to garnish

Chile lamb

Heat the oil in a large, heavy-bottom skillet or flameproof casserole. Add the onion and cook over low heat, stirring occasionally, for 10 minutes, or until golden.

Meanwhile, place the garlic, ginger, ground coriander, chili powder, turmeric, and salt in a small bowl and mix well. Add the spice mixture to the skillet and cook, stirring constantly, for 2 minutes. Add the lamb and cook, stirring frequently, for 8–10 minutes, or until it is broken up and browned.

Add the tomatoes and their juices, the mint, peas, carrots, chile, and fresh cilantro. Cook, stirring constantly, for 3–5 minutes, then serve, garnished with fresh mint sprigs.

serves 4

1 tbsp curry paste
2 fresh green chiles, chopped
5 dried red chiles
2 tbsp tomato paste
2 garlic cloves, chopped
1 tsp chili powder
pinch of sugar
pinch of salt
2 tbsp peanut or corn oil
½ tsp cumin seeds
1 onion, chopped

2 curry leaves
1 tsp ground cumin
1 tsp ground coriander
½ tsp ground turmeric
14 oz/400 g canned chopped tomatoes
⅔ cup chicken stock
4 skinless, boneless chicken breasts
1 tsp garam masala
freshly cooked rice, to serve
fresh mint sprigs, to garnish

Red hot chile chicken

To make the chili paste, place the curry paste, fresh and dried chiles, tomato paste, garlic, chili powder, and sugar in a blender or food processor with the salt. Process to a smooth paste.

Heat the oil in a large, heavy-bottom pan. Add the cumin seeds and cook over medium heat, stirring constantly, for 2 minutes, or until they begin to pop and release their aroma. Add the onion and curry leaves and cook, stirring, for 5 minutes.

Add the chili paste, cook for 2 minutes, then stir in the ground cumin, coriander, and turmeric and cook for an additional 2 minutes.

Add the tomatoes and their juices and the stock. Bring to a boil, then reduce the heat and simmer for 5 minutes. Add the chicken and garam masala, cover, and simmer gently for 20 minutes, or until the chicken is cooked through and tender. Serve immediately with rice and garnished with fresh mint sprigs.

33. Curry Powder

serves 4

2 tsp butter

1 large onion, finely chopped

2 lb/900 g zucchini, sliced

2 cups chicken or vegetable stock

1 tsp curry powder

½ cup sour cream, plus extra to garnish

salt and pepper

Curried zucchini soup

Melt the butter in a large saucepan over medium heat. Add the onion and cook for about 3 minutes, until it begins to soften.

Add the zucchini, stock, and curry powder, along with a large pinch of salt, if using unsalted stock. Bring the soup to a boil, reduce the heat, cover, and cook gently for about 25 minutes, until the vegetables are tender.

Let the soup cool slightly, then transfer to a food processor or blender, working in batches, if necessary. Process the soup until just smooth, but still with green flecks. (If using a food processor, strain off the cooking liquid and reserve. Process the soup solids with enough cooking liquid to moisten them, then combine with the remaining liquid.)

Return the soup to the rinsed-out saucepan and stir in the sour cream. Reheat gently over a low heat just until hot. (Do not boil.)

Taste and adjust the seasoning, if needed. Ladle into warmed bowls, garnish with a swirl of sour cream, and serve.

serves 6

4 tbsp olive oil

2 lb/900 g skinless, boneless chicken meat, diced

⅔ cup diced, rindless, smoked bacon

12 shallots, sliced

2 garlic cloves, chopped finely

1 tbsp curry powder

1¼ cups mayonnaise

1 tbsp honey

1 tbsp chopped fresh flat-leaf parsley

pepper

cold saffron rice, to serve

Coronation chicken

Heat the oil in a large skillet and add the chicken, bacon, shallots, garlic, and curry powder. Cook slowly, stirring, for about 15 minutes.

Spoon the mixture into a clean mixing bowl. Let cool completely, then season to taste with pepper.

Blend the mayonnaise with the honey, then add the parsley. Toss the chicken mixture in the mayonnaise mixture.

Place the chicken in a serving dish, and serve with cold saffron rice.

3

makes 24

heaping ¾ cup all-purpose flour,
  plus extra for dusting

pinch of salt

1 tsp curry powder

4 tbsp butter, plus extra for greasing

½ cup grated cheddar cheese

1 egg, beaten

poppy and cumin seeds, for sprinkling

Cheese straws

Sift the flour, salt, and curry powder into a bowl. Add the butter and rub
in until the mixture resembles breadcrumbs. Add the cheese and half
the egg and mix to form a dough. Wrap in plastic wrap and chill in the
refrigerator for 30 minutes.

Preheat the oven to 400°F/200°C, then grease several cookie sheets.
On a floured counter, roll out the dough to ¼ inch/5 mm thick. Cut into
3 x ½-inch/7.5 x 1-cm strips. Pinch the strips lightly along the sides and
place on the prepared cookie sheets.

Brush the strips with the remaining egg and sprinkle half with poppy
seeds and half with cumin seeds. Bake in the preheated oven for
10–15 minutes, or until golden. Transfer to wire racks to cool.

4

serves 4

4 ripe plantains

1 tsp mild, medium, or hot curry powder,
   to taste

vegetable oil or peanut oil, for deep-frying

mango chutney, to serve

Plantain chips

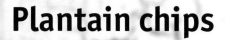

Peel the plantains, then cut crosswise into ⅛-inch/3-mm slices. Put the slices in a bowl, sprinkle over the curry powder, and use your hands to toss them lightly together.

Heat enough oil for deep-frying in a wok, deep-fat fryer, or large heavy-bottom pan to 350°F/180°C, or until a cube of bread browns in 30 seconds. Add as many plantain slices as will fit in the pan without overcrowding and cook for 2 minutes, or until golden.

Remove the plantain chips from the pan with a slotted spoon and drain well on crumpled paper towels. Repeat until all the plantain slices have been fried. Serve hot with mango chutney.

34. Spicy Sausage

serves 6

2 tbsp vegetable oil

1 lb 2 oz/500 g chicken breasts,
  cut into strips

9 oz/250 g spicy sausage, skinned and
  sliced

2 onions, chopped

4 garlic cloves, chopped

1 green bell pepper, seeded and chopped

3 celery stalks, chopped

1 scotch bonnet chile, carefully chopped

3 cups chicken stock

2½ cups long-grain rice

1 lb/450 g large cooked shrimp or crayfish

salt

Jambalaya

Heat the oil in large saucepan, then add the chicken and sausage
and brown for 5 minutes over high heat. Reduce the heat and add
the onions, garlic, bell pepper, and celery and sauté for an additional
10 minutes, until softened. Add the chile and the stock and stir in the
rice. Cover and simmer very gently for 40 minutes.

Add the shrimp and cook for an additional 5 minutes. Check the
seasoning, adding salt to taste. Transfer to warmed bowls and serve.

serves 4

4 tbsp pizza sauce

4 whole-wheat or white English
  muffins, halved

2 tbsp pitted and chopped olives

3 button mushrooms, finely sliced

3½ oz/100 g spicy sausage, skinned
  and sliced

4½ oz/125 g mozzarella cheese,
  thinly sliced

Meat feast muffin pizzas

Spread the pizza sauce over the cut sides of the halved muffins. Sprinkle
over the olives, mushrooms, and spicy sausage.

Lay the mozzarella over the toppings and place under the broiler for
8–10 minutes, or until the cheese is melting.

3

serves 4

4¾ oz/125 g dried conchiglie (pasta shells)

2 tbsp olive oil

1 medium onion, chopped

2 garlic cloves, finely chopped

1 small yellow bell pepper, seeded and cut into thin sticks

6 oz/175 g spicy sausage, skinned and sliced

2 tbsp red wine

1 tbsp red wine vinegar

4 oz/125 g mixed salad greens

salt

Spicy sausage & pasta salad

Bring a large pan of lightly salted water to a boil over medium heat. Add the pasta and cook for 8–10 minutes, or according to the package instructions. Drain and set aside.

Heat the oil in a pan over medium heat. Add the onion and cook until translucent, then stir in the garlic, yellow bell pepper, and sausage and cook for 3–4 minutes, stirring once or twice.

Add the wine, wine vinegar, and reserved pasta to the pan, stir, and bring the mixture just to a boil over medium heat.

Arrange the salad greens on serving plates, spoon over the warm sausage-and-pasta mixture, and serve immediately.

serves 4

3 tbsp olive oil

5 lb/2.25 kg chicken, cut into
  8 pieces and dusted with flour

7 oz/200 g spicy sausage, skinned and
  sliced

small bunch of fresh sage leaves

1 onion, chopped

6 garlic cloves, sliced

2 celery stalks, sliced

1 small pumpkin or butternut squash,
  peeled and roughly chopped

1 cup dry sherry

2½ cups chicken stock

14 oz/400 g canned chopped tomatoes

2 bay leaves

salt and pepper

1 tbsp chopped fresh flat-leaf parsley

Chicken & spicy sausage casserole

Preheat the oven to 350°F/180°C.

Heat the oil in a casserole dish and fry the chicken with the sausage
and sage leaves, until golden brown. Remove with a slotted spoon and
reserve. You may need to do this in two batches.

Add the onion, garlic, celery, and pumpkin and cook until the mixture
begins to brown slightly.

Add the sherry, chicken stock, tomatoes, and bay leaves, and season
with salt and pepper to taste.

Return the reserved chicken, sausage, and sage to the casserole, cover,
and cook in the oven for 1 hour.

Remove the casserole from the oven, uncover, stir in the chopped
parsley, and serve.

35. Almonds

serves 4

2½ cups water

1 onion, finely chopped

1 celery stalk, finely chopped

1 carrot, grated

4 garlic cloves, chopped or crushed

1 bay leaf

½ tsp salt

scant 1 cup ground almonds

2 ripe avocados (about 1 lb/450 g)

3–4 tbsp fresh lemon juice

chopped fresh chives, to garnish

Avocado & almond soup

Combine the water, onion, celery, carrot, garlic, bay leaf, and salt in a saucepan. Bring to a boil, reduce the heat, cover, and simmer for about 30 minutes, or until the vegetables are very tender.

Strain the mixture, reserving the liquid and the vegetables separately. Remove and discard the bay leaf.

Put the vegetables into a blender or food processor. Add the almonds and a small amount of the liquid and process to a very smooth puree, scraping down the sides as necessary. Add as much of the remaining liquid as the capacity of the blender or processor permits and process to combine. Scrape into a bowl, stir in any remaining liquid, cover, and chill until cold.

Cut the avocados in half, discard the pits, and scoop the flesh into the blender or food processor. Add the cold soup and process to a smooth puree, scraping down the sides as necessary. For a thinner consistency, add a few spoonfuls of cold water.

Add the lemon juice and season with salt to taste. Ladle into chilled small bowls and sprinkle each serving lightly with chopped chives.

serves 6

dough

¾ cup salted butter, softened

¼ cup superfine sugar

1 egg yolk

1½ cups all-purpose flour, sifted, plus extra for dusting

filling

1 unwaxed orange

9 tbsp butter

1 cup superfine sugar

2 eggs, beaten

1 heaping cup ground almonds

heavy cream, whipped, to serve

Orange & almond tart

To make the dough, beat the butter and sugar together in a bowl until light and fluffy. Add the egg yolk and stir until fully incorporated and smooth. Gradually add the flour and mix until the dough forms a ball, being careful to avoid overworking it. Divide in half and wrap each half in plastic wrap. Freeze one half and let the other half rest at room temperature for about 20 minutes.

Roll the dough out on a floured work surface and use to line an 8-inch/20-cm tart pan with a removable bottom. Refrigerate until required.

Preheat the oven to 350°F/180°C.

To make the filling, put the orange into a microwave-proof bowl and add a little water to the bowl. Cover with plastic wrap and cook in a microwave oven for 6–7 minutes on high until the orange is completely soft. Alternatively, put the orange in a saucepan, then cover with water and simmer for 40 minutes, or until completely soft. Let the softened orange cool slightly, then cut in half and remove the seeds. Put in a food processor and blend to a puree. Add the butter, sugar, eggs, and almonds and blend again until smooth.

Spoon the mixture into the tart shell and bake in the preheated oven for 40 minutes, or until the filling is firm. Remove from the oven and let cool. Serve the tart in slices with cream.

3

serves 8

butter, for greasing
1 heaping cup ricotta cheese
4 eggs, separated
1 tsp almond extract
generous ¾ cup sugar
2¾ cups ground almonds
finely grated rind of 1 lime
toasted slivered almonds, to decorate
confectioners' sugar, sifted, for dusting

Rich almond cake

Preheat the oven to 300°F/150°C. Grease and line a 9-inch/23-cm round cake pan.

Beat together the ricotta, egg yolks, almond extract, and sugar. Stir in the almonds and lime rind.

Whisk the egg whites in a clean bowl until they form soft peaks.

Fold the whites lightly into the ricotta mixture, using a large metal spoon.

Spread the batter in the pan and bake in the preheated oven for 50–60 minutes, until firm and lightly browned.

Cool the cake in the pan for 10 minutes, then turn out onto a wire rack and sprinkle with slivered almonds and sugar. Let cool completely.

4

serves 6–8

2 slices white bread, crusts removed

3 tbsp water

1 lb/450 g freshly ground pork

1 large onion, chopped

1 garlic clove, crushed

2 tbsp chopped fresh
    flat-leaf parsley, plus extra to garnish

1 egg, beaten

freshly grated nutmeg

all-purpose flour, for coating

2 tbsp Spanish olive oil

lemon juice, to taste

salt and pepper

chopped parsley, to garnish

almond sauce

2 tbsp olive oil

1 slice white bread

scant 1 cup blanched almonds

2 garlic cloves, finely chopped

⅔ cup dry white wine

1¾ cups vegetable stock

Meatballs in almond sauce

For the meatballs, place the bread in a bowl, then add the water and let soak for 5 minutes. Squeeze out the water and return to a dry bowl. Add the ground pork, onion, garlic, parsley, and egg, then season with grated nutmeg and a little salt and pepper. Knead the ingredients to form a smooth mixture. Spread some flour on a plate. With floured hands, shape the meat mixture into about 30 equal balls, then roll each meatball in flour until coated. Heat the oil in a large, heavy-bottom skillet. Add the meatballs, in batches, and cook for 4–5 minutes. Using a slotted spoon, remove the meatballs from the skillet and reserve.

To make the sauce, heat the olive oil in a skillet. Break the bread into pieces, add to the skillet with the almonds, and cook gently, stirring, until golden brown. Add the garlic and fry for 30 seconds, then pour in the wine and boil for 1–2 minutes. Season to taste with salt and pepper and let cool slightly. Transfer to a food processor. Pour in the vegetable stock and process the mixture until smooth. Return the sauce to the skillet.

Add the meatballs to the sauce and simmer for 25 minutes. Taste the sauce and season with salt and pepper, if necessary. Transfer to a serving dish, then add a squeeze of lemon juice to taste and sprinkle with chopped parsley. Serve immediately.

36. Cashew Nuts

serves 4

1½ tbsp peanut oil

1¾ cups snow peas

12–15 baby corn

1 large orange or yellow bell pepper, seeded and thinly sliced

8 scallions, halved lengthwise

2 garlic cloves, well crushed

¾-inch/2-cm piece ginger, peeled and finely chopped

2 tbsp teriyaki marinade

¾ cup unsalted cashew nuts

14 oz/400 g cooked, peeled jumbo shrimp

1 tbsp sesame oil

Teriyaki shrimp with cashew nuts

Heat a large non-stick wok or skillet over high heat. Heat the oil, then add all the vegetables and stir-fry over high heat for 4 minutes, or until almost tender but still with a bite. Add the garlic and ginger and stir-fry for 1 minute.

Add the teriyaki marinade, cashew nuts, and shrimp and stir-fry for 2 minutes.

Serve immediately, with the sesame oil drizzled over.

serves 4

1 tbsp cornstarch

½ tsp five-spice powder

4 turkey steaks, cut into thin strips

1 tsp soy sauce

1 tsp dry sherry

3 tbsp peanut oil

1 garlic clove, finely chopped

1-inch/2.5-cm piece fresh ginger, finely chopped

4 scallions, cut into thin strips

1 large carrot, cut into thin strips

⅔ cup unsalted cashew nuts

2 tbsp hoisin sauce

½ tsp salt

shredded scallions, to garnish

cooked rice, to serve

Turkey & cashew nut stir-fry

Mix together the cornstarch and five-spice powder in a bowl and stir in the turkey. Add the soy sauce and sherry, stirring to coat. Set aside for 30 minutes.

Heat a wok or large skillet over high heat. Heat 2 tablespoons of the oil, then add the turkey mixture and stir-fry for 2–3 minutes, until golden and cooked through. Using a slotted spoon, transfer the turkey to a plate and keep warm.

Heat the remaining oil in the wok and stir-fry the garlic, ginger, scallions, and carrot for 1 minute. Return the turkey to the wok with the cashew nuts, hoisin sauce, and salt. Reduce the heat to medium–high and stir-fry for an additional minute. Sprinkle with shredded scallions and serve immediately with cooked rice.

3

serves 4

1 tbsp butter
2 tbsp olive oil
1 red onion, chopped
¾ cup medium-grain paella rice
1 tsp ground turmeric
1 tsp ground cumin
½ tsp chili powder
3 garlic cloves, crushed
1 fresh green chile, sliced
1 green bell pepper, seeded and diced
1 red bell pepper, seeded and diced

16 baby corn, halved lengthwise
2 tbsp pitted black olives
1 large tomato, seeded and diced
2 cups vegetable stock
heaping ½ cup unsalted
   cashew nuts
scant ½ cup frozen peas
2 tbsp chopped fresh parsley, plus
   extra sprigs to garnish
pinch of cayenne pepper
salt and pepper

Spicy cashew nut paella

Melt the butter with the oil in a paella pan or wide, shallow skillet and cook the onion over medium heat, stirring, for 2–3 minutes, or until softened.

Add the rice, turmeric, cumin, chili powder, garlic, chile, bell peppers, baby corn, olives, and tomato and cook, stirring constantly, for 1–2 minutes. Pour in the stock and bring to a boil. Reduce the heat and cook, stirring frequently, for 20 minutes.

Add the nuts and peas and cook, stirring occasionally, for 5 minutes. Season to taste with salt and pepper and sprinkle with the chopped parsley and cayenne pepper. Transfer to warmed serving plates, then garnish with parsley sprigs and serve immediately.

4

serves 4

2 tbsp peanut oil or vegetable oil

2 red onions, cut into wedges

1 small head cauliflower, cut into florets

1 small head broccoli, cut into florets

2 tbsp prepared yellow curry paste or
  red curry paste

1¾ cups canned coconut milk

1 tsp Thai fish sauce

1 tsp jaggery or dark brown sugar

1 tsp salt

½ cup unsalted cashew nuts

handful of fresh cilantro, chopped, plus
  extra sprigs, torn, to garnish

Cauliflower, broccoli & cashew nut salad

Heat the oil in a preheated wok. Add the onions and stir-fry over medium–high heat for 3–4 minutes, or until starting to brown. Add the cauliflower and broccoli and stir-fry for 1–2 minutes. Stir in the curry paste and stir-fry for 30 seconds, then add the coconut milk, fish sauce, jaggery, and salt. Bring gently to a boil, stirring occasionally, then reduce the heat and simmer gently for 3–4 minutes, or until the vegetables are almost tender.

Meanwhile, heat a separate dry skillet until hot. Add the cashews and cook, shaking the skillet frequently, for 2–3 minutes, or until lightly browned. Add to the stir-fry with the cilantro and stir well, then serve immediately, garnished with torn sprigs of cilantro.

37. Peanut Butter

serves 4

4 skinless, boneless chicken breasts, about 4 oz/115 g each, cut into ¾-inch/2-cm cubes

4 tbsp soy sauce

1 tbsp cornstarch

2 garlic cloves, finely chopped

1-inch/2.5-cm piece fresh ginger, peeled and finely chopped

cucumber cubes, to serve

peanut sauce

2 tbsp peanut or vegetable oil

½ onion, finely chopped

1 garlic clove, finely chopped

4 tbsp crunchy peanut butter

4–5 tbsp water

½ tsp chili powder

Chicken satay skewers with peanut sauce

Put the chicken in a shallow dish. Mix the soy sauce, cornstarch, garlic, and ginger together in a small bowl and pour over the chicken. Cover and let marinate in the refrigerator for at least 2 hours. Meanwhile, soak 12 wooden skewers in cold water for at least 30 minutes.

Preheat the oven to 375°F/190°C. Divide the chicken cubes among the skewers. Heat a ridged grill pan until hot, then add the skewers and cook over high heat for 3–4 minutes, turning occasionally, until browned all over. Transfer the skewers to a baking sheet and cook in the preheated oven for 5–8 minutes, or until cooked through.

Meanwhile, to make the sauce, heat the oil in a pan, then add the onion and garlic and cook over medium heat, stirring frequently, for 3–4 minutes, or until softened. Add the peanut butter, water, and chili powder and simmer for 2–3 minutes, or until softened and thinned.

Serve the skewers immediately with the warm sauce and the cucumber.

serves 3

2 carrots, peeled

2 celery stalks

1 cucumber

3 duck breasts, 5 oz/140 g each

peanut sauce

2 garlic cloves, crushed

2 tbsp dark brown sugar

2 tbsp crunchy peanut butter

2 tbsp coconut cream

2 tbsp soy sauce

2 tbsp rice vinegar

2 tbsp sesame oil

½ tsp freshly ground black pepper

½ tsp Chinese five-spice powder

½ tsp ground ginger

Duck salad with peanut sauce

Preheat the broiler. Cut the carrots, celery, and cucumber into thin strips and set aside.

Broil the duck breasts for about 5 minutes on each side until cooked through. Let cool.

Meanwhile, heat all the ingredients for the sauce in a small pan until combined and the sugar has dissolved completely. Stir until smooth.

Slice the duck breasts and arrange between 3 serving bowls. Place the reserved carrots, celery, and cucumber around the duck, drizzle with the sauce, and serve immediately.

3

makes 26

½ cup butter, softened,
   plus extra for greasing
scant ½ cup crunchy peanut butter
heaping ½ cup superfine sugar
heaping ½ cup light brown sugar
1 egg, beaten
½ tsp vanilla extract
⅔ cup all-purpose flour
½ tsp baking soda
½ tsp baking powder
pinch of salt
1½ cups rolled oats

Crunchy peanut butter cookies

Preheat the oven to 350°F/180°C. Grease 3 cookie sheets.

Place the butter and peanut butter in a bowl and beat together. Beat in the superfine sugar and brown sugar, then gradually beat in the egg and vanilla extract.

Sift the flour, baking soda, baking powder, and salt into the bowl with the peanut butter mixture and stir in the oats until combined.

Place spoonfuls of the cookie dough onto the cookie sheets, spaced well apart to allow for spreading. Flatten slightly with a fork.

Bake in the preheated oven for 12 minutes, or until lightly browned. Let cool on the cookie sheets for 2 minutes, then transfer to wire racks to cool completely.

makes 20

10½ oz/300 g milk chocolate

2½ cups all-purpose flour

1 tsp baking powder

1 cup butter

1¾ cups light brown sugar

2 cups rolled oats

½ cup chopped mixed nuts

1 egg, beaten

14 oz/400 g canned sweetened
    condensed milk

⅓ cup crunchy peanut butter

Chocolate peanut butter squares

Preheat the oven to 350°F/180°C.

Finely chop the chocolate. Sift the flour and baking powder into a large bowl. Add the butter to the flour mixture and rub in using your fingertips until the mixture resembles breadcrumbs. Stir in the sugar, rolled oats, and chopped nuts.

Put a quarter of the batter into a bowl and stir in the chocolate. Set aside.

Stir the egg into the remaining batter, then press into the bottom of a 12 x 8-inch/30 x 20-cm cake pan. Bake in the preheated oven for 15 minutes.

Meanwhile, mix the condensed milk and peanut butter together. Pour into the cake pan and spread evenly, then sprinkle the reserved chocolate mixture on top and press down lightly.

Return to the oven and bake for an additional 20 minutes, until golden brown. Let cool in the pan, then cut into squares.

38. Chocolate

serves 8

¾ cup butter, softened,
    plus extra for greasing
generous 1 cup superfine sugar
3 eggs, beaten
3 tbsp dark corn syrup
3 tbsp ground almonds
generous 1 cup self-rising flour
pinch of salt
¼ cup unsweetened cocoa

frosting
8 oz/225 g semisweet chocolate, broken
    into pieces
¼ cup dark brown sugar
1 cup butter, diced
5 tbsp evaporated milk
½ tsp vanilla extract

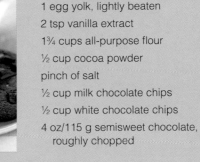

makes 12

1 cup butter, softened
⅔ cup superfine sugar
1 egg yolk, lightly beaten
2 tsp vanilla extract
1¾ cups all-purpose flour
½ cup cocoa powder
pinch of salt
½ cup milk chocolate chips
½ cup white chocolate chips
4 oz/115 g semisweet chocolate,
    roughly chopped

Chocolate fudge cake

Grease and line the bottoms of two 8-inch/20-cm round layer cake pans.

To make the frosting, place the chocolate, brown sugar, butter, evaporated milk, and vanilla extract in a heavy-bottom pan. Heat gently, stirring continuously, until melted. Pour into a bowl and let cool. Cover and let chill in the refrigerator for 1 hour, or until spreadable.

Preheat the oven to 350°F/180°C. Place the butter and superfine sugar in a bowl and beat together until light and fluffy. Gradually beat in the eggs. Stir in the corn syrup and ground almonds. Sift the flour, salt, and cocoa into a separate bowl, then fold into the cake batter. Add a little water, if necessary, to make a dropping consistency.

Spoon the cake batter into the prepared pans and bake in the preheated oven for 30–35 minutes, or until springy to the touch and a skewer inserted in the center comes out clean.

Let stand in the pans for 5 minutes, then turn out onto wire racks to cool completely. When the cakes have cooled, sandwich them together with half the frosting. Spread the remaining frosting over the top and sides of the cake, swirling it to give a frosted appearance.

Mega chip cookies

Preheat the oven to 375°F/190°C. Line 2–3 cookie sheets with parchment paper.

Put the butter and sugar into a bowl and mix well with a wooden spoon, then beat in the egg yolk and vanilla extract. Sift together the flour, cocoa, and salt into the batter, add both kinds of chocolate chips, and stir until thoroughly combined.

Make 12 balls of the batter, put them on the prepared cookie sheets, spaced well apart, and flatten slightly. Press the pieces of semisweet chocolate into the batter.

Bake in the preheated oven for 12–15 minutes. Let cool on the cookie sheets for 5–10 minutes, then carefully transfer to wire racks to cool completely.

3

serves 8

½ cup superfine sugar

½ cup margarine, plus extra for greasing

2 eggs, lightly beaten

3½ oz/100 g ¾ cup all-purpose flour

1 tsp baking powder

2 tbsp unsweetened cocoa

finely pared strips of orange rind,
   to decorate

mousse

7 oz/200 g semisweet chocolate
   (about 70 percent cocoa solids)

grated rind of 2 oranges and juice of 1

4 eggs, separated

Chocolate orange mousse cake

Preheat the oven to 350°F/180°C. Grease and line the bottom of a 9-inch/23-cm round, loose-bottom cake pan with parchment paper. Cream the sugar and margarine together in a mixing bowl until pale and fluffy. Gradually add the eggs, beating well with a wooden spoon between each addition. Sift the flour, baking powder, and cocoa together, fold half into the egg batter, then fold in the remainder. Spoon the batter into the cake pan and level the surface with the back of a spoon. Bake for 20 minutes until risen and firm to the touch. Let cool in the pan.

Meanwhile, make the mousse. Melt the chocolate in a bowl placed over a pan of gently simmering water, making sure that the bottom of the bowl does not touch the water. Let cool, then stir in the orange rind and juice and the egg yolks.

Whisk the egg whites in a large bowl until they form stiff peaks. Gently fold a large spoonful of the egg whites into the chocolate mixture, then fold in the remainder. Spoon the mixture on top of the cooked, cooled sponge and level the top with the back of a spoon. Place in the refrigerator to set. Remove the sides of the pan (though not the bottom) before decorating with the orange rind strips and serving.

4

serves 9

½ cup butter, plus extra for greasing

4 oz/115 g semisweet chocolate, broken into pieces

1⅓ cups superfine sugar

pinch of salt

1 tsp vanilla extract

2 eggs

1 cup all-purpose flour

2 tbsp unsweetened cocoa

½ cup white chocolate chips

fudge sauce

4 tbsp butter

generous 1 cup superfine sugar

⅔ cup milk

generous 1 cup heavy cream

⅓ cup dark corn syrup

7 oz/200 g semisweet chocolate, broken into pieces

Double chocolate brownies

Preheat the oven to 350°F/180°C. Grease a 7-inch/18-cm square cake pan and line the bottom with parchment paper.

Place the butter and chocolate in a small heatproof bowl set over a saucepan of gently simmering water until melted, making sure that the bottom of the bowl does not touch the water. Stir until smooth. Let cool slightly. Stir in the sugar, salt, and vanilla extract. Add the eggs, one at a time, stirring well, until blended.

Sift the flour and cocoa into the cake batter and beat until smooth. Stir in the chocolate chips, then pour the batter into the prepared pan. Bake in the preheated oven for 30–35 minutes, or until the top is evenly colored and a skewer inserted into the center comes out almost clean. Let cool slightly while you prepare the sauce.

To make the sauce, place the butter, sugar, milk, cream, and corn syrup in a small saucepan and heat gently until the sugar has dissolved. Bring to a boil and stir for 10 minutes, or until the mixture is caramel-colored. Remove from the heat and add the chocolate. Stir until smooth. Cut the brownies into squares and serve immediately with the sauce.

39. Maple Syrup

makes 10–12 slices

13 oz/375 g store-bought flaky pastry

6 tbsp all-purpose flour, plus extra for rolling the dough

3 tbsp light brown sugar

3 cups plus 2 tbsp heavy cream

¾ cup maple syrup

2 eggs

4 tsp lemon juice

¾ tsp salt

¼ tsp ground nutmeg

2 tbsp confectioners' sugar

Maple-cream tart

Preheat the oven to 400°F/200°C. Roll out the dough on a lightly floured surface and use to line a 9-inch/23-cm loose-bottom tart pan. Line the dough with wax paper and cover with pie weights or dried beans. Place on a baking sheet and bake in the preheated oven for 15–20 minutes, until golden at the edges.

Meanwhile, combine the flour and sugar in a large bowl. Beat 2 cups of the cream in another bowl with the maple syrup, eggs, lemon juice, salt, and nutmeg. Slowly whisk this mixture into the flour, whisking until no lumps remain.

When the pastry shell is golden, remove the paper and weights and reduce the oven temperature to 350°F/180°C. Pour the filling into the pastry shell, return to the oven, and bake for 30–35 minutes, until set. Remove the tart from the oven and let cool completely on a wire rack.

Whip the remaining cream until soft peaks form. Sift over the confectioners' sugar and continue whipping until stiff. Just before serving, spread the whipped cream over the surface of the tart. Cut into slices to serve.

makes 16

4 oz/115 g bittersweet chocolate, broken into pieces

¾ cup unsalted butter

1¼ cups superfine sugar

4 eggs, beaten

1 tsp vanilla extract

1¾ cups all-purpose flour

¾ cup shelled pistachio nuts, skinned and chopped

glaze

4 oz/115 g bittersweet chocolate, broken into pieces

½ cup sour cream

2 tbsp maple syrup

Maple-glazed brownies

Preheat the oven to 375°F/190°C. Lightly grease a 12 x 8-inch/30 x 20-cm shallow cake pan.

Place the chocolate with the butter in a small pan over low heat and stir until melted. Remove from the heat and stir in the sugar. Whisk the eggs and vanilla extract together in a large bowl until pale. Beat in the melted chocolate mixture. Fold in the flour evenly, then stir in ½ cup of the pistachios.

Spoon into the prepared pan and smooth the top level. Bake for 25–30 minutes, or until firm and golden brown.

For the glaze, melt the chocolate in a heatproof bowl set over a saucepan of gently simmering water, making sure that the bottom of the bowl does not touch the water. Stir in the sour cream and maple syrup and beat until smooth and glossy.

Spread the glaze over the brownies evenly with a metal spatula. Sprinkle with the remaining pistachios and let stand until the topping is set. Cut into squares.

3

makes 18

½ cup butter, softened, plus extra
  for greasing
½ cup pecans
2 tbsp maple syrup
scant ½ cup light brown sugar
1 large egg yolk, lightly beaten
generous ¾ cup self-rising flour

Pecan & maple cookies

Preheat the oven to 375°F/190°C. Lightly grease 2 cookie sheets.
Reserve 18 pecan halves and roughly chop the rest.

Place the butter, maple syrup, and sugar in a bowl and beat together
with a wooden spoon until light and fluffy. Beat in the egg yolk. Sift
over the flour and add the chopped pecans. Mix to a stiff dough.

Place 18 golf ball-size spoonfuls of the batter onto the cookie sheets,
spaced well apart. Top each with a reserved pecan, pressing
down gently.

Bake in the preheated oven for 10–12 minutes, until light golden brown.
Let the cookies cool on the cookie sheets for 10 minutes, then transfer to
a cooling rack and let cool completely.

4

serves 4–6

6 eggs

¾ cup milk

¼ tsp ground cinnamon

12 slices day-old challah or
plain white bread

about 4 tbsp butter or margarine,
plus extra to serve

½ –1 tbsp sunflower-seed or corn oil

salt

warm maple syrup, to serve

French toast with maple syrup

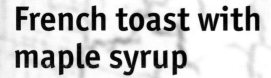

Preheat the oven to 275°F/140°C. Break the eggs into a large, shallow
bowl and beat together with the milk, cinnamon, and salt to taste. Add
the bread slices and press them down so that they are covered on both
sides with the egg mixture. Let the bread stand for 1–2 minutes to soak
up the egg mixture, turning the slices over once.

Melt half the butter with ½ tablespoon of oil in a large skillet. Add
to the pan as many bread slices as will fit in a single layer and cook
for 2–3 minutes, until golden brown.

Turn the bread slices over and cook until golden brown on the other side.
Transfer the French toast to a plate and keep warm in the oven while
cooking the remaining bread slices, adding extra oil if necessary.

Serve the French toast with the remaining butter melting on top and warm
maple syrup for pouring over.

40. Honey

serves 4

3 tbsp butter

3 tbsp honey

scant 4 cups diced winter squash

1 tsp finely chopped fresh thyme

salt and pepper

fresh thyme sprigs, to garnish

serves 4

about 6 oz/175 g goat cheese, such
as Monte Enebro, in one piece

about ⅓ cup honey

⅔ cup walnut halves, chopped

Honey-glazed sautéed squash

Put the butter and honey in a nonstick skillet and heat gently until
melted. Add the squash cubes, chopped thyme, and salt and
pepper and mix well. Sauté over medium heat for 8–10 minutes,
turning and tossing frequently, until the squash cubes are tender
and glazed all over (the glaze will gradually thicken and coat them).

Garnish with thyme sprigs and serve as an appetizer with fresh
bread, or as an accompaniment with broiled chicken, red meat,
or fish.

Goat cheese with honey & walnuts

Remove the cheese from the refrigerator at least 20 minutes before
serving to let it come to room temperature.

Pour the honey into a bowl. Place the walnuts in another bowl.

Serve the cheese on a board with a cheese knife and let everyone cut a
slice for themselves. They then drizzle some honey over, with a dipper,
if available, and sprinkle with chopped walnuts.

Alternatively, cut the cheese into 4 slices and place a slice on each of
4 serving plates. Drizzle some honey over, sprinkle with chopped nuts,
and serve.

serves 4

pasta

generous 2¾ cups type 00 pasta flour
or all-purpose flour

4 eggs, beaten

semolina, for dusting

salt

filling

1 lb 2 oz/500 g sweet potatoes, peeled
and cut into chunks

3 tbsp olive oil

1 large onion, finely chopped
1 garlic clove, crushed

1 tsp fresh thyme leaves, chopped

2 tbsp honey

salt and pepper

sage butter

3-4 tbsp butter

1 bunch fresh sage leaves finely
chopped, reserving a few leaves,
for garnish

Sweet potato ravioli

To make the pasta, sift the flour into a large bowl or food processor. Add the eggs and bring the mixture together or process to make a soft but not sticky dough. Turn out onto a work surface lightly dusted with semolina and knead for 4–5 minutes, or until smooth. Cover with plastic wrap and refrigerate for at least 30 minutes.

For the filling, peel the sweet potatoes and cut into chunks. Cook in a saucepan of boiling water for 20 minutes, or until tender. Drain and mash.

Heat the oil in a skillet over medium heat, then add the onion and cook, stirring frequently, for 4–5 minutes, or until softened but not colored. Stir the onion into the mashed potatoes and add the garlic and thyme leaves. Drizzle with the honey and season to taste with salt and pepper. Set aside.

Using a pasta machine, roll the pasta out to a thickness of about 1⅜ inch/1 mm (or use a rolling pin on a work surface lightly dusted with semolina, and plenty of elbow grease). Cut the pasta in half. Place teaspoonfuls of the filling at evenly spaced intervals across one half of the pasta. Brush around the filling with a small amount of water and cover with the second half. Press lightly around the filling to seal the pasta and cut into squares with a sharp knife or pastry wheel. Lay the ravioli out on a sheet of wax paper that has been lightly dusted with semolina.

Bring a large saucepan of salted water to a boil and drop in the ravioli. Cook for 2–3 minutes, until the pasta rises to the surface and is tender but still retaining a little bite.

Meanwhile, for the sage butter, melt the butter with the sage in a small saucepan over gentle heat. Drain the ravioli and immediately toss with the sage butter. Serve immediately, garnished with sage leaves.

serves 8

scant ¾ cup unsalted butter, plus extra
    for greasing
heaping ½ cup light brown sugar
½ cup honey
1 tbsp lemon juice
2 eggs, beaten
scant 1½ cups self-rising flour
2 tbsp slivered almonds
warmed honey, to glaze

Honey & almond cake

Preheat the oven to 350°F/180°C. Grease and line a deep, 8-inch/ 20-cm
cake pan.

Place the butter, sugar, honey, and lemon juice in a saucepan and stir
over a medium heat, without boiling, until melted and smooth.

Remove the pan from the heat and quickly beat in the eggs with a
wooden spoon. Sift in the flour and stir lightly with a metal spoon. Pour
into the prepared pan and scatter the almonds over the top.

Bake in the preheated oven for 35–40 minutes, until risen, firm, and
golden brown. Cool in the pan for 15 minutes, then turn out onto a wire
rack to cool completely. Drizzle with warmed honey to serve.

41. Raisins

serves 6–8

¼ cup red wine vinegar

2 tbsp superfine sugar

1 bay leaf

pared rind of 1 lemon

scant 1 cup seedless raisins

4 large skinless, boneless chicken breasts, about 1 lb 5 oz/600 g in total

5 tbsp olive oil

1 garlic clove, finely chopped

1 cup pine nuts

⅓ cup extra virgin olive oil

1 small bunch of fresh flat-leaf parsley, finely chopped

salt and pepper

Chicken salad with raisins & pine nuts

To make the dressing, put the vinegar, sugar, bay leaf, and lemon rind in a pan and bring to a boil, then remove from the heat. Stir in the raisins and let cool.

When the dressing is cool, slice the chicken breasts widthwise into very thin slices. Heat the olive oil in a large skillet, then add the chicken slices and cook over medium heat, stirring occasionally, for 8–10 minutes, or until lightly browned and tender.

Add the garlic and pine nuts and cook, stirring constantly and shaking the skillet, for 1 minute, or until the pine nuts are golden brown. Season to taste with salt and pepper.

Pour the cooled dressing into a large bowl, discarding the bay leaf and lemon rind. Add the extra virgin olive oil and whisk together. Season to taste with salt and pepper. Add the chicken mixture and parsley and toss together. Turn the salad into a serving dish and serve warm or, if serving cold, cover and chill in the refrigerator for 2–3 hours before serving.

serves 6

2 tbsp sunflower oil

2 onions, thinly sliced

2 apples, peeled, cored, and thinly sliced

2 lb/900 g red cabbage, cored and shredded

4 tbsp red wine vinegar

2 tbsp sugar

¼ tsp ground cloves

⅓ cup raisins

½ cup red wine

2 tbsp red currant jelly

salt and pepper

Braised red cabbage with raisins

Heat the oil in a large saucepan. Add the onions and cook, stirring occasionally, for 10 minutes, or until softened and golden. Stir in the apple slices and cook for 3 minutes.

Add the cabbage, vinegar, sugar, cloves, raisins, and red wine, and season to taste with salt and pepper. Bring to a boil, stirring occasionally. Reduce the heat, cover, and cook, stirring occasionally, for 40 minutes, or until the cabbage is tender and most of the liquid has been absorbed.

Stir in the red currant jelly, transfer the cabbage to a warmed dish, and serve.

3

serves 6–8

1 cup unsalted butter, plus extra for greasing

8 oz/225 g semisweet chocolate

3 tbsp black coffee

⅓ cup soft light brown sugar

a few drops of vanilla extract

2⅔ cups crushed graham crackers

¾ cup raisins

⅔ cup chopped walnuts

No-bake chocolate cake

Grease and line a 8 x 4 x 2-inch/20 x 10 x 5-cm loaf pan.

Place the chocolate, butter, coffee, sugar, and vanilla extract in a saucepan over a low heat and stir until the chocolate and butter have melted, the sugar has dissolved, and the mixture is well combined.

Stir in the graham crackers, raisins, and walnuts and stir well.

Spoon the batter into the prepared loaf pan. Let set for 1–2 hours in the refrigerator, then turn out and cut into thin slices to serve.

makes 12

9 oz/250 g rhubarb

½ cup + 1 tbsp butter, melted and cooled

scant ½ cup milk

2 eggs, beaten

1⅓ cups all-purpose flour

2 tsp baking powder

heaping ½ cup superfine sugar

3 tbsp raisins

3 pieces preserved ginger, chopped

Rhubarb & raisin muffins

Preheat the oven to 375°F/190°C. Line a 12-cup muffin pan with paper muffin liners.

Chop the rhubarb into lengths of about ½ inch/1 cm. Pour the melted butter and milk into a large bowl and beat in the eggs. Sift the flour and baking powder together and lightly fold into the wet batter, together with the sugar. Gently stir in the rhubarb, raisins, and preserved ginger.

Spoon the batter into the muffin liners and bake in the preheated oven for 15–20 minutes, or until the muffins are risen and golden and spring back when gently touched in the center with the tip of a finger.

42. Canned Tomatoes

serves 6

10½ oz/300 g sourdough bread

generous ⅓ cup chicken stock

4 tbsp extra virgin olive oil

3 tbsp fresh sage leaves, shredded

4 garlic cloves, peeled and finely chopped

1 lb 12 oz/800 g canned chopped
   tomatoes

1 tsp sugar

1 cup hot water

½ cup grated Parmesan cheese

salt and pepper

Italian tomato soup

Chop the bread into rough chunks, about 1 inch/2.5 cm square. Place a heavy-bottom saucepan over medium heat. Add the stock, oil, and sage and simmer until reduced by half. Add the bread and garlic, increase the heat to high, and fry until all the liquid has been soaked up and the bread begins to become crispy.

Add the tomatoes and sugar, stir, and simmer for 15 minutes. Add hot water to thin the soup to your preferred consistency (it should be thick). Simmer for an additional minute. Taste and add salt and pepper, if necessary.

Ladle into bowls, sprinkle a little Parmesan cheese on top, and serve.

serves 4

2 tbsp olive oil

2 onions, chopped

2 garlic cloves, finely chopped

1 tbsp shredded fresh basil

1 lb 12 oz/800 g canned chopped
   tomatoes

1 tbsp tomato paste

10–12 dried cannelloni tubes

butter, for greasing

1 cup ricotta cheese

4 oz/115 g cooked ham, diced

1 egg

½ cup freshly grated Pecorino
   Romano cheese

salt and pepper

Ham & ricotta cannelloni

Preheat the oven to 350°F/180°C. Heat the oil in a large heavy-bottom skillet. Add the onions and garlic and cook over a low heat, stirring occasionally, for 5 minutes, or until the onion is softened. Add the basil, tomatoes and their can juices, and tomato paste and season to taste with salt and pepper. Reduce the heat and simmer for 30 minutes, or until thickened.

Meanwhile, bring a large heavy-bottom saucepan of lightly salted water to a boil. Add the cannelloni tubes, return to a boil and cook for 8–10 minutes, or according to the package instructions. Using a slotted spoon, transfer the cannelloni tubes to a large plate and pat dry with paper towels.

Grease a large, shallow ovenproof dish with butter. Mix the ricotta, ham, and egg together in a bowl and season to taste with salt and pepper. Using a teaspoon, fill the cannelloni tubes with the ricotta mixture and place in a single layer in the dish. Pour the tomato sauce over the cannelloni and sprinkle with the grated Pecorino cheese. Bake in the preheated oven for 30 minutes, or until golden brown. Serve immediately.

3

serves 6

3 lb 5 oz/1.5 kg mussels

3 tbsp olive oil

2 onions, chopped

3 garlic cloves, finely chopped

1 red bell pepper, seeded and sliced

3 carrots, chopped

1 lb 12 oz/800 g canned chopped tomatoes

½ cup dry white wine

2 tbsp tomato paste

1 tbsp chopped fresh dill

2 tbsp chopped fresh parsley

1 tbsp chopped fresh thyme

1 tbsp fresh basil leaves, plus extra to garnish

2 lb/900 g white fish fillets, cut into chunks

1 lb/450 g shrimp

1½ cups fish stock or water

salt and pepper

Fishermen's stew

Clean the mussels by scrubbing or scraping the shells and pulling off any beards. Discard any with broken shells and any that refuse to close when tapped with a knife. Rinse the mussels under cold running water.

Heat the oil in a flameproof casserole. Add the onions, garlic, bell pepper, and carrots and cook over low heat, stirring occasionally, for 5 minutes, or until softened.

Add the tomatoes and their juices, the white wine, tomato paste, dill, parsley, and thyme, and tear in the basil leaves. Bring to a boil, then reduce the heat and simmer for 20 minutes.

Add the chunks of fish, mussels, shrimp, and stock and season to taste with salt and pepper. Return the stew to a boil and simmer for 6–8 minutes, or until the shrimp have turned pink and the mussel shells have opened. Discard any shells that remain closed.

Serve immediately, garnished with basil leaves.

4

serves 4

pizza dough

3½ cups all-purpose flour, plus extra
   for dusting

2 tsp salt

2 tsp active dry yeast

2 tbsp olive oil, plus extra for brushing

¾ cup lukewarm water

filling

½ cup olive oil

1 red onion, thinly sliced

1 garlic clove, finely chopped

14 oz/400 g canned chopped tomatoes

⅓ cup pitted and chopped black olives

7 oz/200 g mozzarella cheese, drained
   and diced

1 tbsp chopped fresh oregano

salt and pepper

Calzone pizza turnovers

To make the pizza dough, sift the flour and salt into a bowl and stir in the
yeast. Make a well in the center and pour in the oil and water. Gradually
incorporate the dry ingredients into the liquid, using a wooden spoon or
floured hands.

Turn out the dough onto a lightly floured counter and knead well for 5 minutes,
or until smooth and elastic. Return to the clean bowl, cover with lightly oiled
plastic wrap, and set aside to rise in a warm place for 1 hour, or until doubled
in size.

Meanwhile, preheat the oven to 400°F/200°C. To make the filling, heat the
olive oil in a skillet. Add the onion and garlic and cook over low heat, stirring
occasionally, for 5 minutes, or until softened. Add the tomatoes and cook,
stirring occasionally, for an additional 5 minutes. Stir in the olives and season
to taste with salt and pepper. Remove the pan from the heat.

Divide the dough into 4 pieces. Roll out each piece on a lightly floured counter
to form an 8-inch/20-cm circle.

Divide the tomato mixture among the circles, spreading it over half of each
circle, almost to the edge. Top with the cheese and sprinkle with the oregano.
Brush the edge of each circle with a little water and fold over the uncovered
sides. Press the edges to seal.

Transfer the turnovers to lightly oiled cookie sheets and bake in the preheated
oven for 15 minutes, or until golden and crisp. Remove from the oven and let
stand for 2 minutes, then transfer to warmed plates and serve.

Keep me dry   189

43. Kidney Beans

serves 4–6

1½ cups dried kidney beans
1 tbsp olive oil
2 onions, finely chopped
4 garlic cloves, finely chopped
1 celery stalk, thinly sliced
1 carrot, halved and thinly sliced
5 cups water
2 tsp tomato paste
⅛ tsp dried thyme
⅛ tsp dried oregano
⅛ tsp ground cumin
1 bay leaf
14 oz/400 g canned chopped tomatoes
9 oz/250 g peeled pumpkin flesh, diced
¼ tsp chili paste, or to taste
salt and pepper

Kidney bean, pumpkin & tomato soup

Pick over the beans, cover generously with cold water, and let soak for 6 hours, or overnight. Drain the beans, put in a saucepan, and add enough cold water to cover by 2 inches/5 cm. Bring to a boil and simmer for 10 minutes. Drain and rinse well.

Heat the oil in a large saucepan over medium heat. Add the onions, cover, and cook for 3–4 minutes, until they are just softened, stirring occasionally. Add the garlic, celery, and carrot, and continue cooking for 2 minutes.

Add the water, drained beans, tomato paste, thyme, oregano, cumin, and bay leaf. When the mixture begins to bubble, reduce the heat to low. Cover and simmer gently for 1 hour, stirring occasionally.

Stir in the tomatoes, pumpkin, and chili paste and continue simmering for an additional hour, or until the beans and pumpkin are tender, stirring from time to time.

Season to taste with salt and pepper and stir in a little more chili paste, if desired. Ladle the soup into bowls and serve.

serves 4–6

6 oz/175 g mixed salad greens
1 red onion
1 cup cherry tomatoes
2 cooked beets
¾ cup thinly sliced radishes
1 cup canned cannellini beans, drained and rinsed
¾ cup canned kidney beans, drained and rinsed
1 cup canned flageolets, drained and rinsed
scant ⅓ cup dried cranberries
scant ½ cup roasted cashew nuts
about 2 cups drained feta cheese, crumbled

Three bean salad with feta cheese

Arrange the salad greens in a salad bowl and set aside.

Cut the onion in half and thinly slice to form semicircles. Put into a bowl.

Cut the tomatoes in half and peel the beets, if necessary, and dice. Add to the onion with the remaining ingredients, except the nuts and cheese.

Sprinkle over the nuts and cheese and serve at once.

3

serves 4

4 tbsp olive oil

1 onion, chopped

2 garlic cloves, finely chopped

scant 1 cup brown rice

2½ cups vegetable stock

1 red bell pepper, seeded and chopped

2 celery stalks, sliced

8 oz/225 g cremini mushrooms, thinly
    sliced

15 oz/425 g canned kidney beans, drained
    and rinsed

3 tbsp chopped fresh parsley, plus extra
    to garnish

⅓ cup cashew nuts

salt and pepper

Kidney bean risotto

Heat half the oil in a large, heavy-bottom saucepan. Add the onion and cook, stirring occasionally, for 5 minutes, or until softened. Add half the garlic and cook, stirring frequently, for 2 minutes, then add the rice and stir for 1 minute, or until the grains are thoroughly coated with the oil. Add the stock and a pinch of salt and bring to a boil, stirring constantly. Reduce the heat, cover, and simmer for 35–40 minutes, or until all the liquid has been absorbed.

Meanwhile, heat the remaining oil in a heavy-bottom skillet. Add the bell pepper and celery and cook, stirring frequently, for 5 minutes. Add the sliced mushrooms and the remaining garlic and cook, stirring frequently, for 4–5 minutes.

Stir the rice into the skillet. Add the beans, parsley, and cashew nuts. Season with salt and pepper to taste and cook, stirring constantly, until piping hot. Transfer to a warmed serving dish, sprinkle with extra parsley, and serve.

makes 4

1 tbsp sunflower oil, plus extra for brushing

1 onion, finely chopped

1 garlic clove, finely chopped

1 tsp ground coriander

1 tsp ground cumin

2 cups finely chopped white mushrooms

15 oz/425 g canned kidney beans, drained and rinsed

2 tbsp chopped fresh flat-leaf parsley

all-purpose flour, for dusting

salt and pepper

crusty rolls and salad, to serve

Bean burgers

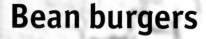

Heat the oil in a heavy-bottom skillet over medium heat. Add the onion and cook, stirring frequently, for 5 minutes, or until softened. Add the garlic, coriander, and cumin and cook, stirring, for an additional minute. Add the mushrooms and cook, stirring frequently, for 4–5 minutes, until all the liquid has evaporated. Transfer to a bowl.

Put the beans in a small bowl and mash with a fork. Stir into the mushroom mixture with the parsley and season to taste with salt and pepper.

Preheat the broiler to medium-high. Divide the mixture equally into 4 portions, dust lightly with flour, and shape into flat, round burgers. Brush with oil and cook under the broiler for 4–5 minutes on each side. Serve in crusty rolls with salad.

44. Lima Beans

serves 4

- 2 tbsp olive oil
- 1 onion, chopped
- 2 celery stalks, chopped
- 1 large carrot, coarsely chopped
- 1 large or 2 small sweet potatoes, peeled and chopped
- 1 cup drained and rinsed canned lima beans
- 4 cups vegetable stock
- 1 large handful fresh cilantro leaves
- 2 tbsp freshly grated Parmesan cheese
- salt and pepper

serves 2

- 1 tbsp olive oil
- 1 small onion, finely diced
- 1 garlic clove, crushed
- ½ cup drained and rinsed canned lima beans
- ⅓ cup water
- 1 tbsp tomato paste
- 1 tsp balsamic vinegar
- 1 tbsp chopped fresh parsley
- 1 tbsp torn fresh basil
- salt and pepper
- slices ciabatta bread, toasted, to serve

Sweet potato & lima bean soup

Heat the oil in a large saucepan over medium heat, then add the onion, celery, and carrot and cook, stirring frequently, for 8–10 minutes, or until softened. Add the sweet potatoes and beans and cook, stirring, for 1 minute.

Add the stock, then stir thoroughly and bring to a simmer. Season with a little salt and pepper to taste. Cover, then reduce the heat and cook for 25–30 minutes, or until all the vegetables are tender.

Let cool slightly, then transfer one-third of the soup to a blender or food processor and blend until smooth. Return to the saucepan and mix in well. Adjust the salt and pepper, if necessary and reheat.

Ladle into warmed bowls and scatter with the cilantro and Parmesan cheese before serving.

Lima beans on ciabatta toast with fresh herbs

Heat the oil in a medium sauté pan and cook the onion over low heat until soft. Add the garlic and cook for an additional 1 minute, then add the lima beans, water, and tomato paste. Bring to a boil, stirring occasionally, and cook for 2 minutes.

Add the balsamic vinegar, parsley, and basil and stir to combine. Season to taste with salt and pepper and serve over slices of toasted ciabatta.

serves 4

2 tbsp olive oil

1 tbsp fresh thyme leaves

4 large sea bass fillets,
    about 6 oz/175 g each

salt and pepper

cherry tomatoes on the vine, for serving

lima bean puree

3 tbsp olive oil

2 garlic cloves, chopped

2½ cups drained and rinsed canned lima
    beans

juice of 1 lemon

2–3 tbsp water

4 tbsp chopped fresh flat-leaf parsley

Baked sea bass with lima bean puree

Preheat the oven to 400°F/200°C. Mix the oil, thyme, and a little salt and pepper to taste together in a small bowl or pitcher. Arrange the sea bass fillets on a baking sheet, then pour over the oil mixture and carefully turn to coat well. Put the baking sheet on the top shelf of the preheated oven and bake for 15 minutes.

Meanwhile, make the bean puree. Heat the oil in a saucepan over a medium heat, then add the garlic and cook, stirring, for 1 minute. Add the beans and heat through for 3–4 minutes, then add the lemon juice and a little salt and pepper to taste. Transfer to a blender or food processor, then add the water and blend lightly until you have a puree. Alternatively, mash thoroughly with a fork. Stir the parsley into the puree.

Serve the sea bass fillets on top of the warm bean purée with a drizzle of any pan juices. Serve with vine tomatoes.

4

serves 4

1 large onion, chopped

½ cup drained and rinsed canned lima beans

½ cup drained and rinsed canned kidney beans

½ cup drained and rinsed canned chickpeas

2 zucchini, coarsely chopped

2 large carrots, coarsely chopped

4 tomatoes, peeled and coarsely chopped

2 celery stalks, trimmed and chopped

1¼ cups vegetable stock

2 tbsp tomato paste

salt and pepper

crumble topping

1¾ cups whole-wheat breadcrumbs

¼ cup hazlenuts, finely chopped

heaping 1 tbsp chopped fresh parsley

1 cup grated cheddar cheese

Mixed bean & vegetable crumble

Preheat the oven to 350°F/180°C.

Put the onion, lima beans, kidney beans, chickpeas, zucchini, carrots, tomatoes, and celery in a large ovenproof saucepan. Mix together the stock and tomato paste and pour over the vegetables. Season to taste with salt and pepper. Transfer to the preheated oven and bake for 15 minutes.

Meanwhile, to make the crumble topping, put the breadcrumbs in a large bowl, add the hazelnuts, chopped parsley, and grated cheese, and mix together well.

Remove the vegetables from the oven and carefully sprinkle over the crumble topping. Do not press it down or it will sink into the vegetables.

Return to the oven and bake for 30 minutes, or until the crumble topping is golden brown. Remove from the oven and serve hot.

43. Canned Tuna

1

serves 4

3 tbsp red pesto

1 store-bought pizza crust,
   12 inches/30 cm wide

7 oz/200 g canned tuna in brine, drained

12 cherry tomatoes, halved

scant 1 cup diced
   mozzarella cheese

2 tbsp capers

8 small pitted black olives

1 tbsp olive oil

salt and pepper

Speedy tuna pizza

Preheat the oven to 425°F/220°C. Place the pizza crust on a baking sheet, then spread the pesto evenly over the top.

Coarsely flake the tuna and arrange over the pizza.

Scatter over the tomatoes, mozzarella, capers, and olives. Season to taste with salt and pepper.

Drizzle the oil over the pizza and bake in the preheated oven for about 15 minutes, or until golden and bubbling.

2

makes 4 fishcakes

4 tbsp all-purpose flour

7 oz/200 g canned tuna in brine,
   drained

2–3 tbsp curry paste

1 scallion, trimmed and finely
   chopped

1 egg, beaten

sunflower or peanut oil, for frying

salt and pepper

arugula leaves, to serve

Spicy tuna fishcakes

Mix the flour with plenty of salt and pepper on a large flat plate. Mash the tuna with the curry paste, scallion, and beaten egg in a large bowl.

Form into 4 patties and dust with the seasoned flour.

Heat the oil in a skillet, add the patties, and fry for 3–4 minutes on each side, until crisp and golden. Serve on a bed of arugula leaves.

3

serves 4–6

7 oz/200 g dried ribbon egg pasta, such as tagliatelle

2 tbsp butter

1 cup fine fresh breadcrumbs

14 fl oz/400 ml canned condensed cream of mushroom soup

½ cup milk

2 celery stalks, chopped

1 red bell pepper, seeded and chopped

1 green bell pepper, seeded and chopped

1¼ cups coarsely grated sharp cheddar cheese

2 tbsp chopped fresh parsley

7 oz/200 g canned tuna in brine, drained, and flaked

salt and pepper

Tuna & noodle casserole

Preheat the oven to 400°F/200°C. Bring a large pan of salted water to a boil. Add the pasta, then return to a boil and cook for 2 minutes less than specified on the package instructions.

Meanwhile, melt the butter in a separate small pan. Stir in the breadcrumbs, then remove from the heat and set aside.

Drain the pasta well and set aside. Pour the soup into the pasta pan and set over medium heat, then stir in the milk, celery, bell peppers, half the cheese, and all the parsley. Add the tuna and gently stir in so that the flakes don't break up. Season to taste with salt and pepper. Heat just until small bubbles appear around the edge of the mixture—do not boil.

Stir the pasta into the pan and use 2 forks to mix all the ingredients together. Spoon the mixture into an ovenproof dish that is also suitable for serving and spread it out.

Stir the remaining cheese into the buttered breadcrumbs, then sprinkle over the top of the pasta mixture. Bake in the preheated oven for 20–25 minutes, or until the topping is golden. Remove from the oven, then let stand for 5 minutes before serving straight from the dish.

4

serves 2

1 tbsp plain yogurt

1 tsp olive oil

½ tsp white wine vinegar

½ tsp Dijon mustard

1 large egg, hard-cooked and cooled

7 oz/200 g canned tuna in brine drained, and flaked

scant 1 cup canned corn kernels

2 whole wheat flour tortillas

1 container fine curled cress or alfalfa sprouts

pepper

Tuna, egg & corn wraps

To make the dressing, whisk the yogurt, oil, vinegar, and mustard, and pepper to taste in a pitcher until emulsified and smooth.

Shell the egg, separate the yolk and the white, then mash the yolk and mince the white. Mash the tuna with the egg and dressing, then mix in the corn.

Spread the filling equally over the 2 tortillas and sprinkle over the cress. Fold in one end and roll up.

46. Anchovies

serves 4

3½ oz/100 g canned anchovy fillets

3 cups black olives, pitted and coarsely chopped

2 garlic cloves, coarsely chopped

2 tbsp capers in brine, drained and rinsed

1 tbsp Dijon mustard

3 tbsp extra virgin olive oil

2 tbsp lemon juice

Tapenade

Drain the anchovies, reserving the oil from the can. Coarsely chop the fish and place in a food processor. Add the reserved oil and all the remaining ingredients. Process to a smooth paste. Stop and scrape down the sides of the food processor, if necessary.

Transfer the tapenade to a dish, cover with plastic wrap, and chill in the refrigerator until required. If you are not planning to use the tapenade until the following day (or even the one after), cover the surface with a layer of olive oil to prevent it from drying out.

serves 4

1 large egg

2 romaine lettuce or 3 Boston lettuce

2 tbsp lemon juice

8 canned anchovy fillets, drained and coarsely chopped

¾ cup fresh Parmesan cheese shavings

salt and pepper

garlic croutons

⅔ cup olive oil

2 garlic cloves

5 slices white bread, crusts removed, cut into ½-inch/1-cm cubes

Caesar salad

Bring a small, heavy-bottom pan of water to a boil.

Meanwhile to make the croutons, heat 4 tablespoons of the olive oil in a heavy-bottom skillet. Add the garlic and cubed bread and cook, stirring and tossing frequently, for 4–5 minutes, or until the bread is crispy and golden all over. Remove from the skillet with a slotted spoon and drain on paper towels.

Add the egg to the boiling water and cook for 1 minute, then remove from the pan and set aside.

Arrange the lettuce in a salad bowl. Mix together the remaining olive oil and lemon juice, then season to taste with salt and pepper. Crack the egg into the dressing and whisk to blend. Pour the dressing over the lettuce, toss well, then add the croutons and chopped anchovies and toss the salad again. Sprinkle with Parmesan cheese shavings and serve.

serves 4

2 lb/900 g fresh baby spinach leaves

14 oz/400 g dried fettuccine

5 tbsp olive oil

3 tbsp pine nuts

3 garlic cloves, crushed

8 canned anchovy fillets,
    drained and chopped

salt

Anchovy & spinach pasta with pine nuts

Trim off any tough spinach stalks. Rinse the spinach leaves under cold running water and place them in a large pan with only the water that is clinging to them after washing. Cover and cook over high heat, shaking the pan from time to time, until the spinach has wilted but retains its color. Drain well, set aside, and keep warm.

Bring a large, heavy-bottom pan of lightly salted water to a boil. Add the fettuccine, return to a boil, and cook for 8–10 minutes, or according to the package instructions.

Heat 4 tablespoons of the olive oil in a separate pan. Add the pine nuts and cook until golden. Remove the pine nuts from the pan and set aside until needed.

Add the garlic to the pan and cook until golden. Add the anchovies and stir in the spinach. Cook, stirring, for 2–3 minutes, until heated through. Return the pine nuts to the pan.

Drain the fettuccine, toss in the remaining olive oil, and transfer to a warmed serving dish. Spoon the anchovy and spinach sauce over the fettuccine, toss lightly, and serve immediately.

4

makes 40

2 oz/55 g canned anchovies fillets in olive
oil, drained and coarsely chopped

⅓ cup pitted and chopped black olives

1 cup finely grated Manchego or cheddar
cheese

3/4 cup all-purpose flour,
plus extra for dusting

½ cup unsalted butter, diced

½ tsp cayenne pepper,
plus extra for dusting

Anchovy, olive &
cheese triangles

Place all the ingredients in a food processor and pulse until a dough
forms. Turn out and shape into a ball. Wrap in plastic wrap and let chill in
the refrigerator for 30 minutes.

Preheat the oven to 400°F/200°C. Unwrap the dough, knead on a
lightly floured counter, and roll out thinly. Using a sharp knife, cut it into
strips about 2 inches/5 cm wide. Cut diagonally across each strip to
make triangles.

Arrange the triangles on 2 baking sheets and dust lightly with cayenne
pepper. Bake in the preheated oven for 10 minutes, or until golden
brown. Transfer to wire racks to cool completely.

47. Black Olives

serves 4

a few grape leaves
4 tomatoes, sliced
½ cucumber, peeled and sliced
1 small red onion, sliced thinly
1 cup feta cheese, cubed
8 black olives, pitted

dressing

3 tbsp extra virgin olive oil
1 tbsp lemon juice
½ tsp dried oregano
salt and pepper

serves 6–8

⅔ cup pitted black olives
⅔ cup butter, softened
4 tbsp chopped fresh parsley
4 skinless, boneless chicken breasts

Greek feta salad

To make the dressing, put the oil, lemon juice, oregano, and salt and pepper to taste in a screw-top jar and shake together until blended.

Arrange the grape leaves on a serving dish and then the tomatoes, cucumber, and onion. Sprinkle the cheese and olives on top. Pour the dressing over the salad and serve.

Chicken rolls with olives

Preheat the oven to 400°F/200°C. Pit and finely chop the olives. Mix the olives, butter, and parsley together in a bowl.

Place the chicken breasts between 2 sheets of plastic wrap and beat gently with a meat mallet or the side of a rolling pin.

Remove from plastic wrap and spread the olive-and-herb butter over one side of each flattened chicken breast and roll up. Secure with a wooden toothpick or tie with clean string if necessary.

Place the chicken rolls in an ovenproof dish. Drizzle over the oil from the olive jar and bake in the preheated oven for 45–55 minutes, or until tender and the juices run clear when the chicken is pierced with the point of a sharp knife.

Transfer the chicken rolls to a cutting board and discard the toothpicks or string. Using a sharp knife, cut into slices, then transfer to warmed serving plates and serve.

makes 2 loaves

3½ cups all-purpose flour,
    plus extra for dusting

1 tsp salt

1 envelope active dry yeast

1 tsp brown sugar

1 tbsp chopped fresh thyme

scant 1 cup lukewarm water

4 tbsp olive oil, plus extra for brushing

½ cup pitted and sliced black olives

½ cup pitted and sliced green olives

1¾ cups sliced, drained sun-dried
    tomatoes in oil

1 egg yolk, beaten

Olive & sun-dried tomato bread

Sift the flour and salt together into a bowl and stir in the yeast, sugar, and thyme. Make a well in the center and pour in the lukewarm water and oil. Stir well with a wooden spoon until the dough begins to come together, then knead with your hands until it leaves the side of the bowl. Turn out onto a lightly floured counter and knead in the olives and sun-dried tomatoes, then knead for 5 minutes more, until the dough is smooth and elastic.

Brush a bowl with oil. Shape the dough into a ball, put it into the bowl, and put the bowl into a plastic bag or cover with a damp dish towel. Let rise in a warm place for 1–1½ hours, until the dough has doubled in volume.

Dust a cookie sheet with flour. Turn out the dough onto a lightly floured counter and punch down. Cut it in half and with lightly floured hands, shape each half into a round or oval. Put them on the prepared cookie sheet and put the cookie sheet into a plastic bag or cover with a damp dish towel. Let rise in a warm place for 45 minutes.

Preheat the oven to 400°F/200°C. Make 3 shallow diagonal slashes on the top of each loaf and brush with the beaten egg yolk. Bake for 40 minutes, until golden brown and the loaves sound hollow when tapped on the bottom with your knuckles. Transfer to a wire rack to cool.

4

serves 8

3 lb 5 oz–4 lb 8 oz/1.5–2 kg boned lamb shoulder, trimmed of fat and chopped into 1½-inch/4-cm cubes

4 tbsp olive oil

2 cups pitted dates

2 cups pitted black olives

3 cups red wine

10 whole garlic cloves, peeled

large handful of fresh cilantro, chopped

couscous mixed with lemon zest and thyme leaves, to serve

dry marinade

2 large Bermuda onions, grated

4 garlic cloves, crushed

1 red chile, seeded and finely chopped

1 tsp paprika

2 tsp ground cumin

1 tsp ground ginger

1 tsp pepper

Lamb tagine with dates & olives

Combine all the dry marinade ingredients in a casserole dish, add the lamb, and let marinate in the refrigerator for 4 hours or overnight.

Preheat the oven to 300°F/150°C. Remove the lamb from the refrigerator. Add all the remaining ingredients, except the cilantro, to the casserole and cover. Transfer to the preheated oven and cook for 2½ hours, removing the lid for the last 30 minutes. Check that the lamb is meltingly tender, stir in the cilantro, and serve with couscous.

48. Onions

serves 6

1 lb 8 oz/675 g onions
3 tbsp olive oil
4 garlic cloves, 3 chopped and 1 halved
1 tsp sugar
2 tsp chopped fresh thyme, plus extra
   sprigs to garnish
2 tbsp all-purpose flour
½ cup dry white wine
8½ cups vegetable stock
6 slices French bread
2½ cups grated Gruyère cheese

makes 12

1 cup chickpea flour
1 tsp salt
1 tsp ground cumin
1 tsp ground turmeric
1 tsp baking soda
½ tsp chili powder
2 tsp lemon juice
2 tbsp vegetable or peanut oil, plus
   extra for deep-frying
2–8 tbsp water
2 onions, thinly sliced
2 tsp coriander seeds, lightly crushed

French onion soup

Thinly slice the onions. Heat the oil in a large, heavy-bottom pan over medium–low heat, add the onions, and cook, stirring occasionally, for 10 minutes, or until they are just beginning to brown. Stir in the chopped garlic, sugar, and chopped thyme, then reduce the heat and cook, stirring occasionally, for 30 minutes, or until the onions are golden brown.

Sprinkle in the flour and cook, stirring constantly, for 1–2 minutes. Stir in the wine. Gradually stir in the stock and bring to a boil, skimming off any foam that rises to the surface, then reduce the heat and simmer for 45 minutes.

Meanwhile, preheat the broiler to medium. Toast the bread on both sides under the broiler, then rub the toast with the cut edges of the halved garlic clove.

Ladle the soup into 6 ovenproof bowls set on a baking sheet. Float a piece of toast in each bowl and divide the grated cheese among them. Place under the broiler for 2–3 minutes, or until the cheese has just melted. Garnish with thyme sprigs and serve immediately.

Onion bhajis

Sift the chickpea flour, salt, cumin, turmeric, baking soda, and chili powder into a large bowl. Add the lemon juice and oil, then gradually stir in just enough water until a batter forms that is similar in consistency to light cream. Mix in the onions and coriander seeds.

Heat enough oil for deep-frying in a wok, deep-fat fryer, or large, heavy-bottom pan until it reaches 350°F/180°C, or until a cube of bread browns in 30 seconds. Without overcrowding the pan, drop in spoonfuls of the onion mixture and cook for 2 minutes, then use tongs to flip the bhajis over and cook for an additional 2 minutes, or until golden brown.

Immediately remove the bhajis from the oil and drain well on crumpled paper towels. Keep the bhajis warm while you continue cooking the remaining batter. Serve hot.

3

serves 4–6

scant ½ cup unsalted butter

1 lb 5 oz/600 g onions, thinly sliced

2 eggs

scant ½ cup heavy cream

scant 1 cup grated Gruyère cheese

8-inch/20-cm store-bought pie crust

scant 1 cup coarsely grated Parmesan cheese

salt and pepper

Caramelized onion tart

Melt the butter in a heavy-bottom skillet over medium heat. Add the onions and cook, stirring frequently to avoid burning, for 30 minutes, or until well-browned and caramelized. Remove the onions from the skillet and set aside.

Preheat the oven to 375°F/190°C. Beat the eggs in a large bowl, stir in the cream, and season to taste with salt and pepper. Add the Gruyère and mix well. Stir in the cooked onions.

Pour the egg-and-onion batter into the baked pie crust and sprinkle with the Parmesan cheese. Put on a baking sheet. Bake in the preheated oven for 15–20 minutes, until the filling has set and begun to brown.

Remove from the oven and let the tart rest for at least 10 minutes. The tart can be served hot or left to cool to room temperature.

serves 4

1 lb/450 g starchy potatoes
1 medium onion, grated
salt and pepper
oil for shallow-frying

Onion rösti

Wash the potatoes, but do not peel them. Place them in a large saucepan, cover with water, and bring to a boil, covered, over high heat. Reduce the heat and simmer for about 10 minutes, until the potatoes are just beginning to soften. Be careful not to overcook.

Drain the potatoes. Cool, then peel and grate coarsely. Mix the grated onion with the potatoes. Season the mixture with salt and pepper.

Heat the oil in a heavy skillet and spoon in the potato mixture. The vegetable cakes can be as thick or as thin as you like, and can be made into 1 large cake or several individual ones.

Cook over high heat for about 5 minutes, until the bottom is golden, then turn and cook until the second side is brown and crispy. Remove from the heat, drain, and then serve.

49. Potatoes

serves 6

2 lb 4 oz/1 kg potatoes

¾ cup butter, plus extra for greasing

2¼ cups milk

1 lb 5 oz/600 g firm whitefish fillets, such as cod or haddock

14 oz/400 g undyed smoked haddock fillet

3 bay leaves

⅓ cup all-purpose flour

handful of fresh parsley, chopped

2 cups cooked, peeled shrimp

4 hard-cooked eggs, shelled and quartered

4 tbsp melted butter

salt and pepper

minted peas, to serve

crusty bread, to serve

Fish pie

Peel and quarter the potatoes. Bring a large saucepan of lightly salted water to a boil, add the potatoes, and cook for 15–20 minutes, or until tender. Drain, mash thoroughly with half the butter and 2 tablespoons of the milk, then season with salt and pepper, cover, and keep warm.

Place the fish fillets in a shallow saucepan and pour over the remaining milk. Add the bay leaves and place over low heat. Bring the milk to a gentle simmer and poach the fish for 4 minutes (the fillets should not be fully cooked because they will be baked later). Remove from the pan and place on a plate, discard the bay leaves, and reserve the milk. Remove any remaining bones and skin from the fish and flake into large chunks. Put in a bowl, cover, and set aside.

Melt the remaining butter in a saucepan, then stir in the flour to make a roux and cook, stirring occasionally, for 3 minutes. Gradually add the reserved milk, a ladleful at a time, and mix into the roux. Add the parsley, the cooked fish, the shrimp, and the eggs. Fold carefully together. Season with salt and pepper to taste.

Preheat the oven to 400°F/200°C. Butter a pie plate and fill it with the fish mixture. Lay the potatoes on top, making a pattern. Drip the melted butter over the whole pie, place in the oven, and bake for 30–40 minutes, until the top is golden brown.

Serve the pie with minted peas and some crusty French baguette.

serves 6

butter, for greasing

1 lb 9 oz/700 g potatoes, peeled and thinly sliced

2 scallions, finely chopped

1 red onion, finely chopped

⅔ cup heavy cream

1 lb fresh prepared puff pastry

2 eggs, beaten

salt and pepper

Potato & red onion pie

Preheat the oven to 400°F/200°C. Lightly grease a cookie sheet. Bring a pan of water to a boil, then add the sliced potatoes. Bring back to a boil and simmer for a few minutes. Drain the potato slices and let cool. Dry off any excess moisture with paper towels.

In a bowl, mix together the scallions, red onion, and the cooled potato slices. Stir in 2 tablespoons of the cream and plenty of salt and pepper.

Divide the pastry in half and roll out one piece to a 9-inch/23-cm circle. Roll the remaining pastry to a 10-inch/25-cm circle.

Place the smaller circle onto the cookie sheet and top with the potato mixture, leaving a 1-inch/2.5-cm border. Brush this border with a little of the beaten egg.

Top with the larger circle of pastry, seal well, and crimp the edges of the pastry. Cut a steam vent in the middle of the pastry and mark with a pattern. Brush with some of the beaten egg and bake in a preheated oven for 30 minutes.

Mix the remaining beaten egg with the rest of the cream and pour into the pie through the steam vent. Return to the oven for 15 minutes, then let cool for 30 minutes. Serve warm or cold.

3

serves 4

4 large potatoes
1¾ cups cubed, cooked chicken
4 scallions, thickly sliced
1 cup soft cheese
pepper
mixed salad, to serve

Baked potatoes with chicken

Preheat the oven to 400°F/200°C. Bake the potatoes in the preheated oven for about 60 minutes, until tender, or cook in a microwave on high power for 12–15 minutes.

Mix the chicken and scallions with the soft cheese.

Cut a cross into the top of each potato and squeeze slightly apart. Spoon the chicken filling into the potatoes and season with pepper. Serve immediately with a mixed salad.

serves 4

2 lb 4 oz/1 kg potatoes
6 tbsp olive oil
2 sprigs fresh rosemary
5½ oz/150 g baby shallots
2 garlic cloves, sliced
salt and pepper

Roasted potato wedges with shallots & rosemary

Preheat the oven to 400°F/200°C. Peel and cut each potato into 8 thick wedges. Put the potatoes in a large saucepan of lightly salted water and bring to the boil. Reduce the heat and simmer for 5 minutes.

Heat the oil in a large roasting pan. Drain the potatoes well and add to the roasting pan. Strip the leaves from the rosemary sprigs, chop finely, and sprinkle over the potatoes.

Roast the potatoes in the preheated oven for 35 minutes, turning twice during cooking. Add the shallots and garlic and roast for an additional 15 minutes, until golden brown. Season to taste with salt and pepper.

Transfer to a warmed serving dish and serve.

50. Apples

serves 6

1 tbsp butter

3 leeks, thinly sliced

1 large carrot, thinly sliced

1 lb 4 oz/550 g sweet potatoes, peeled and cubed

2 large apples, peeled and cubed

5 cups water

freshly grated nutmeg

1 cup apple juice

1 cup whipping or light cream

salt and pepper

snipped fresh chives or cilantro, to garnish

Sweet potato & apple soup

Melt the butter in a large saucepan over medium–low heat. Add the leeks, then cover and cook for 6–8 minutes, or until soft, stirring frequently.

Add the carrot, sweet potatoes, apples, and water to the saucepan and season lightly with salt, pepper, and nutmeg. Bring to a boil, then reduce the heat and simmer, covered, for about 20 minutes, stirring occasionally, until the vegetables are very tender.

Let the soup cool slightly, then transfer to a blender or food processor and puree until smooth, working in batches if necessary. (If using a food processor, strain off the cooking liquid and reserve. Puree the soup solids with enough cooking liquid to moisten them, then combine with the remaining liquid.)

Return the puree soup to the saucepan and stir in the apple juice. Place over low heat and simmer for about 10 minutes, until heated through.

Stir in the cream and continue simmering for about 5 minutes, stirring frequently, until heated through. Taste and adjust the seasoning, adding more salt, pepper, and nutmeg, if necessary. Ladle the soup into warm bowls, then garnish with chives or cilantro and serve.

serves 4

2 large heads of lettuce

9 oz/250 g dried penne (pasta quills)

8 apples

juice of 4 lemons

1 bunch of celery, sliced

¾ cup walnut halves

1 cup fresh garlic mayonnaise

salt

Penne & apple salad

Wash and drain the lettuce leaves, then pat them dry with paper towels. Transfer them to the refrigerator for 1 hour, until crisp.

Meanwhile, bring a large pan of lightly salted water to a boil. Add the pasta, bring back to a boil, and cook for 8–10 minutes, or according to the package instructions. Drain the pasta and refresh under cold running water. Drain thoroughly and set aside.

Core and dice the apples, then place them in a small bowl and sprinkle with the lemon juice. Mix together the pasta, celery, apples, and walnut halves and toss the mixture in the garlic mayonnaise. Add more mayonnaise, to taste.

Line a salad bowl with the lettuce leaves and spoon the pasta salad into the lined bowl. Refrigerate until ready to serve.

3

makes about 7 lb 10 oz/3.5 kg

2 lb/900 g apples, peeled, cored, and
   chopped

1 lb/450 g onions, chopped

1 lb/450 g ripe plums, rinsed, pitted, and
   chopped

rind and juice of 2 lemons (preferably
   unwaxed and organic), scrubbed

2¼ cups fresh cranberries (if fresh are
   unavailable, use dried)

1 lb/450 g brown sugar

4 kiwis, peeled and sliced

2 cups vinegar

2 tbsp balsamic vinegar

Fruity apple chutney

Place the apples, onions, and plums in a large pan with the lemon rind,
juice, and cranberries. Cook over gentle heat, stirring frequently, for
12 minutes, or until the cranberries are beginning to "pop."

Stir in all the remaining ingredients and heat gently, stirring occasionally,
until the sugar has completely dissolved. Bring to a boil, then reduce
the heat and simmer for 35–40 minutes, or until a thick consistency is
reached.

Remove from the heat and let cool slightly, then pot into warmed
sterilized jars. Cover with nonmetallic lids, then label and store in a
cool place.

4

serves 6

⅓ cup all-purpose flour
heaping ⅓ cup cornstarch
pinch of salt
1 tsp baking powder
1 egg
⅔ cup iced water
5 apples, cored and sliced
peanut oil, for deep-frying
superfine sugar, for dusting
vanilla ice cream, to serve

Hot apple fritters

Sift the flour, cornstarch, salt, and baking powder together into a large bowl. Stir in the egg and water and mix to a fairly smooth batter.

Heat the oil in a deep-fat fryer to 350–375°F/180–190°C, or until a cube of bread browns in 30 seconds. Dip the apple slices into the batter, then add to the hot oil and cook until crisp and golden. Remove with a slotted spoon and drain on paper towels.

Dust the apple fritters with superfine sugar and serve immediately with vanilla ice cream.

Index

Aïoli 128
almonds
    Avocado & almond soup 159
    Chocolate fudge cake 171
    Honey & almond cake 181
    Meatballs in almond sauce 161
    Orange & almond tart 159
    Rich almond cake 160
anchovies
    Anchovy, olive & cheese triangles 205
    Anchovy & spinach pasta with pine nuts 204
    Caesar salad 203
    Deep-fried mozzarella 89
    Panzanella 108
    Spaghetti alla puttanesca 20
    Tapenade 203
apples
    Apple pie 77
    Braised red cabbage with raisins 183
    Fruity apple chutney 220
    Homemade turkey burgers 115
    Hot apple fritters 221
    Penne & apple salad 219
    Sweet potato & apple soup 219
    Wine jelly 141
arugula
    Goat cheese salad with balsamic vinegar 131
    Lentil & goat cheese salad 124
    Linguine with smoked salmon & arugula 48
asparagus
    Asparagus & tomato tart 75
    Penne with asparagus & gorgonzola 112
    Smoked salmon salad with avocado 49
avocados
    Avocado & almond soup 159
    Guacamole 95
    Shrimp & avocado wraps 51
    Smoked salmon salad with avocado 49

bacon/pancetta
    Bacon & lentil soup 123
    Bacon & sour cream dip 96
    Bolognese sauce 36
    Broccoli, pancetta & bleu cheese galette 64
    Chicken & potato soup with bacon 45
    Coronation chicken 151
    Crispy spinach & bacon 43
    Lasagne 37
    Leek & bacon tartlets 44
    Mussel & pasta soup 111
    Potato, bacon & garlic gratin 25
    Rice & peas 72
    Spaghetti carbonara 43
    Toasted muffins with blueberries & bacon 27
balsamic vinegar
    Goat cheese salad with balsamic vinegar 131
    Roasted balsamic & honey onions 132
    Rosemary & garlic balsamic vinegar 131
    Strawberry & balsamic vinegar
        semifreddo 133

bananas: Chocolate banana sundae 99
beef
    Beef burgers 35
    Bolognese sauce 36
    Chili con carne 147
    Lasagna 37
    Meatballs 35
    Red wine-braised beef 139
    Reuben sandwich 107
beet
    Cajun chicken salad with mango & beet 41
    Three bean salad with feta cheese 191
bell peppers
    Chicken & vegetable casserole 40
    Eggplant & bell pepper dip 57
    Eggplant curry 55
    Gazpacho 107
    Mozzarella omelet 87
    Mushroom, potato & bell pepper hash 60
    Nachos with jalapeño & cheese 31
    Panzanella 108
    Pepperoni & bell pepper pasta 113
    Pork with peppered noodles 121
    Spicy cashew nut paella 164
    Spicy sausage & mushroom kebabs 61
    Teriyaki shrimp with cashew nuts 163
    Three-color frittata 91
    Tropical rice salad 117
    Tuna & noodle casserole 200
bleu cheese
    Broccoli, pancetta & bleu cheese galette 64
    Penne with asparagus & gorgonzola 112
    Stilton & walnut tartlets 75
blueberries
    Blueberry & passion fruit drizzle squares 28
    Blueberry & vanilla muffins 27
    Spicy blueberry & cinnamon jam 29
    Toasted muffins with blueberries & bacon 27
bread
    Bread & butter pudding 109
    Bruschetta 19
    Caesar salad 203
    Cheese & sun-dried tomato toasts 88
    Crispy spinach & bacon 43
    Deep-fried mozzarella 89
    French toast with maple syrup 177
    Gazpacho 107
    Italian tomato soup 187
    Lima beans on ciabatta toast with fresh
        herbs 195
    Olive & sun-dried tomato bread 208
    Panzanella 108
    Reuben sandwich 107
    Roasted garlic with goat cheese 23
    Scallion & parmesan cornbread 84
    Wild garlic & broccoli crostini 63
    Zucchini & parmesan bread 67
broccoli
    Broccoli, pancetta & bleu cheese galette 64
    Cauliflower, broccoli & cashew nut salad 165

Cauliflower & broccoli tart 65
Chicken & broccoli soup 63
Vegetable stir-fry 120
Vegetables with Chinese noodles 137
Wild garlic & broccoli crostini 63
Bruschetta 19

cabbage
    Braised red cabbage with raisins 183
    Chunky vegetable soup 143
    Green lentil stew 123
    Spring stew 145
Caesar salad 203
Cajun chicken salad with mango & beet 41
Calzone pizza turnovers 189
cannellini beans
    Spring stew 145
    Three bean salad with feta cheese 191
capers
    Panzanella 108
    Spaghetti alla puttanesca 20
    Speedy tuna pizza 199
    Tapenade 203
carrots
    Chunky vegetable soup 143
    Mixed bean & vegetable crumble 197
    Spring stew 145
    Vegetable stir-fry 120
    Zucchini, carrot & tomato frittata 69
cashew nuts
    Cauliflower, broccoli & cashew nut salad 165
    Kidney bean risotto 192
    Spicy cashew nut paella 164
    Teriyaki shrimp with cashew nuts 163
    Three bean salad with feta cheese 191
    Turkey & cashew nut stir-fry 163
cauliflower
    Cauliflower, broccoli & cashew nut salad 165
    Cauliflower & broccoli tart 65
    Cauliflower cheese 80
celery
    Chunky vegetable soup 143
    Penne & apple salad 219
    Spring stew 145
cheddar cheese
    Cauliflower & broccoli tart 65
    Cauliflower cheese 80
    Cheddar biscuits 81
    Cheese straws 152
    Cheesey zucchini & ham gratin 68
    Chicken & vegetable casserole 40
    Ham & cheese croissant 79
    Lasagna 37
    Macaroni cheese 79
    Mixed bean & vegetable crumble 197
    Nachos with jalapeño & cheese 31
    Tuna & noodle casserole 200
cheese
    Anchovy, olive & cheese triangles 205
    Baked potatoes with chicken 216

Caramelized onion tart 212
French onion soup 211
Nachos with jalapeño & cheese 31
Potato, bacon & garlic gratin 25
Reuben sandwich 107
    see also bleu cheese; cheddar cheese;
        feta cheese; mozzarella cheese;
        Parmesan cheese
chicken
    Baked potatoes with chicken 216
    Chicken & broccoli soup 63
    Chicken chow mein 135
    Chicken with 40 garlic cloves 23
    Chicken laksa 39
    Chicken, mint & shallot rice 116
    Chicken noodle soup 119
    Chicken & potato soup with bacon 45
    Chicken rolls with olives 207
    Chicken salad with raisins & pine nuts 183
    Chicken satay skewers with peanut sauce 167
    Chicken soup 39
    Chicken & spicy sausage casserole 157
    Chicken & vegetable casserole 40
    Coronation chicken 151
    Jambalaya 155
    Red hot chile chicken 149
chickpeas: Mixed bean & vegetable crumble 197
chiles
    Chile lamb 148
    Chile roast potatoes 147
    Chili con carne 147
    Guacamole 95
    Hot & sour soup 135
    Hot sesame noodles 119
    Jambalaya 155
    Red hot chile chicken 149
    see also jalapeño chiles
chocolate
    Chocolate banana sundae 99
    Chocolate fudge cake 171
    Chocolate orange mousse cake 172
    Chocolate peanut butter squares 169
    Double chocolate brownies 173
    Maple-glazed brownies 175
    Mega chip cookies 171
    No-bake chocolate cake 184
coconut
    Cauliflower, broccoli & cashew nut salad 165
    Chicken laksa 39
    Chicken noodle soup 119
    Coconut cream 100
    Eggplant curry 55
corn
    Chicken & broccoli soup 63
    Chunky vegetable soup 143
    Egg-fried rice with vegetables 115
    Spicy cashew nut paella 164
    Spring stew 145
    Teriyaki shrimp with cashew nuts 163

Tropical rice salad 117
Tuna, egg & corn wraps 201
Vegetable stir-fry 120
Vegetables with Chinese noodles 137
cornmeal: Scallion & parmesan
cornbread 84
Crab soufflé 91
cranberries: Three bean salad with feta
cheese 191
cucumber
Cold cucumber & smoked salmon soup 47
Gazpacho 107
Greek feta salad 207
curry powder
Cheese straws 152
Coronation chicken 151
Curried zucchini soup 151
Plantain chips 153

dates: Lamb tagine with dates & olives 209
duck
Duck & fava bean risotto 144
Duck salad with peanut sauce 167
Duck & red wine casserole 139

eggplants
Eggplant & bell pepper dip 57
Eggplant curry 55
Eggplant gratin 55
Stuffed eggplant 56
eggs
Aïoli 128
Chive scrambled eggs with brioche 92
Crab soufflé 91
Deep-fried mozzarella 89
Egg-fried rice with vegetables 115
Ginger baked alaskas 99
Lemon meringue pie 76
Mozzarella omelet 87
Shrimp omelet 52
Spaghetti carbonara 43
Three-color frittata 91
Traditional crème brûlée 93
Tuna, egg & corn wraps 201
Zucchini, carrot & tomato frittata 69
Zucchini & thyme fritters 67
extra virgin olive oil
Aïoli 128
Pesto 129
Porcini with parsley & extra virgin olive
oil 127
Spaghetti olio e aglio 127
fava beans: Spring stew 145
fennel: Macaroni & seafood casserole 111
feta cheese
Greek feta salad 207
Three bean salad with feta cheese 191
Fish pie 215
Fishermen's stew 188

flageolets: Three bean salad with feta cheese 191
flaky pastry
French toast with maple syrup 177
Apple pie 77
Asparagus & tomato tart 75
Lemon meringue pie 76
Stilton & walnut tartlets 75

garlic
Aïoli 128
Chicken with 40 garlic cloves 23
Garlic shrimp 51
Potato, bacon & garlic gratin 25
Roasted garlic with goat cheese 23
Roasted pumpkin, garlic & thyme soup 24
Rosemary & garlic balsamic vinegar 131
Sautéed garlic mushrooms 59
Spaghetti olio e aglio 127
Wild garlic & broccoli crostini 63
Gazpacho 107
goat cheese
Goat cheese with honey & walnuts 179
Goat cheese salad with balsamic vinegar 131
Lentil & goat cheese salad 124
Roasted garlic with goat cheese 23
Smoked salmon & goat cheese tarts 47
Guacamole 95

ham
Cheesey zucchini & ham gratin 68
Ham & cheese croissant 79
Ham & ricotta cannelloni 187
honey
Goat cheese with honey & walnuts 179
Honey & almond cake 181
Honey-glazed sautéed squash 179
Roasted balsamic & honey onions 132
Sweet potato ravioli 180
Hot & sour soup 135

jalapeño chiles
Jalapeño bhajis 32
Nachos with jalapeño & cheese 31
Salmon & jalapeño fish cakes 31
Tropical salsa 33
Jambalaya 155

kidney beans
Bean burgers 193
Chili con carne 147
Kidney bean, pumpkin & tomato soup 191
Kidney bean risotto 192
Mixed bean & vegetable crumble 197
Three bean salad with feta cheese 191
kiwis: Fruity apple chutney 220

lamb
Chile lamb 148
Lamb tagine with dates & olives 209

Lasagne 37
leeks
Leek & bacon tartlets 44
Sweet potato & apple soup 219
Lemon meringue pie 76
lentils
Bacon & lentil soup 123
Green lentil stew 123
Lentil & goat cheese salad 124
Spiced lentils with spinach 125
lima beans
Baked sea bass with lima bean purée 196
Lima beans on ciabatta toast with fresh
herbs 195
Mixed bean & vegetable crumble 197
Sweet potato & lima bean soup 195

mangoes: Cajun chicken salad with mango &
beef 41
maple syrup
French toast with maple syrup 177
Maple-cream tart 175
Maple-glazed brownies 175
Pecan & maple cookies 176
Meatballs 35
Meatballs in almond sauce 161
mozzarella cheese
Calzone pizza turnovers 189
Cheese & sun-dried tomato toasts 88
Deep-fried mozzarella 89
Eggplant gratin 55
Meat feast muffin pizzas 155
Meatballs 35
Mozzarella omelet 87
Speedy tuna pizza 199
Stuffed eggplant 56
Stuffed rice balls 87
Three-color salad 19
mushrooms
Chicken & vegetable casserole 40
Chicken chow mein 135
Creamy mushroom & tarragon soup 59
Egg-fried rice with vegetables 115
Hot & sour soup 135
Kidney bean risotto 192
Mushroom, potato & bell pepper hash 60
Porcini with parsley & extra virgin olive oil 127
Pork stroganoff 143
Red wine-braised beef 139
Sautéed garlic mushrooms 59
Spicy sausage & mushroom kebabs 61
Tuna & noodle casserole 200
mussels
Fishermen's stew 188
Mussel & pasta soup 111

Nachos with jalapeño & cheese 31
noodles
Chicken chow mein 135

Chicken laksa 39
Chicken noodle soup 119
Hot sesame noodles 119
Pork with peppered noodles 121
Vegetable stir-fry 120
Vegetables with Chinese noodles 137
nuts
Chocolate banana sundae 99
Chocolate peanut butter squares 169
Maple-glazed brownies 175
Mixed bean & vegetable crumble 197
Pecan & maple cookies 176
see also almonds; cashew nuts; peanut butter;
walnuts

oats
Chocolate peanut butter squares 169
Crunchy peanut butter cookies 168
olives
Anchovy, olive & cheese triangles 205
Calzone pizza turnovers 189
Chicken rolls with olives 207
Deep-fried mozzarella 89
Greek feta salad 207
Lamb tagine with dates & olives 209
Meat feast muffin pizzas 155
Olive & sun-dried tomato bread 208
Spaghetti alla puttanesca 20
Speedy tuna pizza 199
Spicy cashew nut paella 164
Tapenade 203
onions
Caramelized onion tart 212
French onion soup 211
Fruity apple chutney 220
Onion bhajis 211
Onion rösti 213
Peas with pearl onions 73
Potato & red onion pie 215
Roasted balsamic & honey onions 132
oranges
Chocolate orange mousse cake 172
Orange & almond tart 159
Tropical salsa 33

Panzanella 100
Parmesan cheese
Asparagus & tomato tart 75
Caesar salad 203
Caramelized onion tart 212
Crispy Parmesan-coated sea bass 83
Eggplant gratin 55
Italian tomato soup 187
Lasagne 37
Macaroni & seafood casserole 111
Macaroni cheese 79
Meatballs 35
Parmesan & pine nut muffins 85
Pesto 129
Rice & peas 72

Spaghetti carbonara 43
Scallion & parmesan cornbread 84
Stuffed eggplant 56
Stuffed rice balls 87
Summer vegetable & herb tart 83
Three-color frittata 91
Zucchini & parmesan bread 67
parsnips
Chicken soup 39
Chicken & vegetable casserole 40
passion fruit: Blueberry & passion fruit drizzle
squares 28
pasta
Anchovy & spinach pasta with pine nuts 204
Ham & ricotta cannelloni 187
Lasagna 37
Linguine with smoked salmon & arugula 48
Macaroni cheese 79
Macaroni & seafood casserole 111
Mussel & pasta soup 111
Penne & apple salad 219
Penne with asparagus & gorgonzola 112
Pepperoni & bell pepper pasta 113
Spaghetti alla puttanesca 20
Spaghetti carbonara 43
Spaghetti olio e aglio 127
Spicy sausage & pasta salad 156
Stuffed eggplant 56
Sweet potato ravioli 180
Tuna & noodle casserole 200
peanut butter
Chicken noodle soup 119
Chicken satay skewers with peanut sauce 167
Chocolate peanut butter squares 169
Crunchy peanut butter cookies 168
Duck salad with peanut sauce 167
Hot sesame noodles 119
Pears in red wine sauce 140
peas
Chicken noodle soup 119
Chile lamb 148
Chilled pea soup 71
Peas with pearl onions 73
Rice & peas 72
Scallops & pea puree 71
Spicy cashew nut paella 164
Pepperoni & bell pepper pasta 113
Pesto 129
pineapple
Coconut cream 100
Sour cream & pineapple muffins 97
Tropical rice salad 117
Plantain chips 153
pork
Meatballs in almond sauce 161
Paprika pork 95
Pork with peppered noodles 121
Pork stroganoff 143
potatoes
Baked potatoes with chicken 216
Chicken & potato soup with bacon 45
Chile roast potatoes 147

Fish pie 215
Mushroom, potato & bell pepper hash 60
Onion rösti 213
Potato, bacon & garlic gratin 25
Potato & red onion pie 215
Roasted potato wedges with shallots &
rosemary 217
Salmon & jalapeño fish cakes 31
Spring stew 145
pumpkin
Chicken & spicy sausage casserole 157
Kidney bean, pumpkin & tomato soup 191
Roasted pumpkin, garlic & thyme soup 24

raisins
Braised red cabbage with raisins 183
Chicken salad with raisins & pine nuts 183
No-bake chocolate cake 184
Rhubarb & raisin muffins 185
Tropical rice salad 117
red wine
Duck & red wine casserole 139
Pears in red wine sauce 140
Red wine-braised beef 139
Wine jelly 141
refried beans: Nachos with jalapeño &
cheese 31
Rhubarb & raisin muffins 185
rice
Chicken & broccoli soup 63
Chicken, mint & shallot rice 116
Chicken & vegetable casserole 40
Duck & fava bean risotto 144
Egg-fried rice with vegetables 115
Home-made turkey burgers 115
Jambalaya 155
Kidney bean risotto 192
Rice & peas 72
Spicy cashew nut paella 164
Stuffed rice balls 87
Tropical rice salad 117
ricotta cheese
Ham & ricotta cannelloni 187
Rich almond cake 160
Summer vegetable & herb tart 83

salmon
Salmon & jalapeño fish cakes 31
see also smoked salmon
Scallops & pea puree 71
sea bass
Baked sea bass with lima bean purée 196
Crispy Parmesan-coated sea bass 83
shrimp
Fish pie 215
Fishermen's stew 188
Garlic shrimp 51
Jambalaya 155
Macaroni & seafood casserole 111
Shrimp & avocado wraps 51
Shrimp cocktail 53
Shrimp omelet 52

Teriyaki shrimp with cashew nuts 163
smoked salmon
Cold cucumber & smoked salmon soup 47
Linguine with smoked salmon & arugula 48
Smoked salmon & goat cheese tarts 47
Smoked salmon salad with avocado 49
snow peas
Egg-fried rice with vegetables 115
Teriyaki shrimp with cashew nuts 163
sour cream
Bacon & sour cream dip 96
Creamy mushroom & tarragon soup 59
Curried zucchini soup 151
Guacamole 95
Paprika pork 95
Roasted pumpkin, garlic & thyme soup 24
Sour cream & pineapple muffins 97
soy sauce
Chicken chow mein 135
Chicken satay skewers with peanut sauce 167
Duck & noodle salad with peanut sauce 167
Egg-fried rice with vegetables 115
Hot sesame noodles 119
Hot & sour soup 135
Sweet potato cakes with soy-tomato
sauce 136
Vegetables with Chinese noodles 137
spicy sausage
Chicken & spicy sausage casserole 157
Jambalaya 155
Meat feast muffin pizzas 155
Spicy sausage & mushroom kebabs 61
Spicy sausage & pasta salad 156
spinach
Anchovy & spinach pasta with pine nuts 204
Asparagus & tomato tart 75
Crispy spinach & bacon 43
Macaroni cheese 79
Mozzarella omelet 87
Spiced lentils with spinach 125
squash: Honey-glazed sautéed squash 179
Strawberry & balsamic vinegar semifreddo 133
sugar snap peas
Chicken laksa 39
Duck & red wine casserole 139
sweet potatoes
Chicken & vegetable casserole 40
Sweet potato & apple soup 219
Sweet potato cakes with soy-tomato
sauce 136
Sweet potato & lima bean soup 195
Sweet potato ravioli 180

Tapenade 203
tofu
Hot & sour soup 135
Vegetables with Chinese noodles 137
tomatoes
Asparagus & tomato tart 75
Bruschetta 19
Calzone pizza turnovers 189
Cheese & sun-dried tomato toasts 88

Chicken & spicy sausage casserole 157
Chicken & vegetable casserole 40
Chicken laksa 39
Chili con carne 147
Chunky vegetable soup 143
Eggplant gratin 55
Fishermen's stew 188
Gazpacho 107
Greek feta salad 207
Ham & ricotta cannelloni 187
Italian tomato soup 187
Kidney bean, pumpkin & tomato soup 191
Lasagne 37
Meatballs 35
Olive & sun-dried tomato bread 208
Panzanella 108
Pepperoni & bell pepper pasta 113
Red hot chile chicken 149
Spaghetti alla puttanesca 20
Speedy tuna pizza 199
Stuffed eggplant 56
Sweet potato cakes with soy-tomato
sauce 136
Three-color frittata 91
Three-color salad 19
Tomato tarte tatin 21
Zucchini, carrot & tomato frittata 69
tuna
Speedy tuna pizza 199
Spicy tuna fishcakes 199
Tuna, egg & corn wraps 201
Tuna & noodle casserole 200
turkey
Homemade turkey burgers 115
Turkey & cashew nut stir-fry 163
turnips
Bacon & lentil soup 123
Chicken soup 39

vanilla ice cream
Chocolate banana sundae 99
Coconut cream 100
Ginger baked alaskas 99
Ice cream cookie sandwiches 101
vegetable stock
Chunky vegetable soup 143
Duck & fava bean risotto 144
Pork stroganoff 143
Spring stew 145

walnuts
Cajun chicken salad with mango & beet 41
Goat cheese with honey & walnuts 179
No-bake chocolate cake 184
Penne & apple salad 219
water chestnuts: Vegetable stir-fry 120
watermelon: Tropical salsa 33

zucchini
Cheesey zucchini & ham gratin 68
Curried zucchini soup 151
Three-color frittata 91
Zucchini, carrot & tomato frittata 69
Zucchini & parmesan bread 67
Zucchini & thyme fritters 67